DIVINE DICTIONARY FOR DELIVERANCE

Tonida Jacqueline Cooper

TABLE OF CONTENT

DEDICATION

All praises to the most-high Yah, through his son Yahshua for
helping me with completing this book. It has been a long journey,
but Yah kept me. Through all the interruptions, setbacks, hardships,
and discouragements, I made it. Spirits of darkness have tried to do
everything in their power to keep me from completing all books that
released this year. However, Yah kept me and gave me the joy I
needed to research this gloomy information. During the journey, I
learned the reason why I was experiencing the things I had gone
through. Therefore, I had to fast and pray in between writing.
However, the good news is that I believe all the hard work put into
this is not in vain but will set many free that are captive, and Yah
will get all praise for it. Thank you, Yah, HalleluYah!

INTRODUCTION

I will be using the Hebrew names of the Almighty Yah and His son Yahshua. Whenever you see Yah and Yahshua, I am speaking of whom you call God and Jesus.

YAH-meaning **"Self-Existence"** and creator of **ALL**
YAHSHUA-meaning **"Yah is Savior"** (Yah's son)
Ruach Ha Quadash- meaning **"Holy Spirit."**

Halleluyah **Yah**, thank you for the *Messiyah Yahshua*
HalleluYah- Meaning, "Praise you Yah"

Some of you that call the **ALMIGHTY** God, says that he has many names, however, that is incorrect. People confuse Yah's attributes with His name. **For example, some people may think that Yahova Yarah is also His name but it is one of His attributes, meaning He is a provider, but it is not his name.**

The meaning of SIN is the Transgression of **"YAH'S LAWS"** (His word) **1 JOHN 3:4.** Everyone who practices sin also practices lawlessness, and sin is lawlessness [**ignoring Yah's law by action or neglect or by tolerating wrongdoing—being unrestrained by His commands and His will**].

Peace to all readers. The title of this book came to mind as a resource to define what spirits of darkness are causing chaos in people's lives. "Divine Dictionary for Deliverance," list demons and the details of the evil they do that surround us every day that people are not aware of, and how they affect their lives daily. Satan will make something look innocent and fun on the down-low (**hidden**), but the truth of the matter is that he is destroying individuals and their families. **(Proverbs 14:12)**. I pray that this book will deliver those in bondage that is locked in the N'MOS cycle trying to find answers. You will know what the N'MOS cycle means when you get to the page defining the functions of the named demons.

I was miserable for a large number of my life because I did not know that certain demons were sent to oppress me because of covenant agreements made with ancestors associated with demons.

I explain it extensively in my book "**Chosen to Break Generational Curses**." It did not matter how much I love Yah and the anointing that was on me, and evidence of the fruit of the spirit on me. I could not break free until I came to the knowledge that there were demons that had a right to run certain parts of my life because of family members involved in some kind of covenant with Satan and demons and things that I participated in too for a lack of knowledge.

Negative words that were spoken over me as a child and in my young adulthood by those that were in an authoritative position over me were used by demons to help plant a negative complex within me over time. I was conditioned to accept that as the norm for my way of life. However, **SATAN IS A LIAR,** and I am so glad Yah showed me how to be delivered. I renounced that thought and no longer accept that lie from Satan. Until I came into this knowledge, there were times it seemed that no matter how much I love Yah, I was at a point in my life where I was ready to throw in the towel because it seemed I was constantly fighting an uphill battle and it seems that I was not winning in the spiritual realm.

Whether it was my finances, keeping a job for a long period, or having healthy relationships. The more I tried to climb up, the more I kept being knocked back down. Then finally, it seemed a breakthrough would come, and then immediately it seemed a week later there was a sudden shutdown. It continued to happen because of the lack of knowledge regarding spiritual warfare, and the profound effects of generational curses are why I kept losing the battle.

Satan and his demons took advantage of my lack of knowledge about spiritual warfare. However, Yah was still with me every step of the way. Praise you Yah and HalleluYah. I now see why the enemy tried to kill me since birth, and it was because of my divine destiny to reveal this information and my ministry altogether.

I pray that this book will force individuals to identify the problems in their own lives and use the written examples of prayers to be free from them.

During that time, I was searching the bible on how to be free from issues in my life. Yah directed me to read many books with bible references. I also discovered that there was a book removed from the bible with the names of certain demons, and the evil functions they are responsible for in this world. It was amazing what I found out, and I was writing down the ones I needed to cast out of my life. I went on a three-day fast and prayed, and cast out those demons, and it worked.

That is why I wrote this book. After you have read, the evil things that demons are responsible for you should be able to identify with one or two, or maybe more of the listed spirits of darkness, and cast them out to be free. It is not mandatory to know the names, but good to know, so when you are trying to pinpoint what is wrong with you and your life there is a list of named demons to identify issues in your life that you cannot seem to shake.

Some demons are very stubborn so you may have to fast and pray to be delivered. **Do Not Allow Thoughts Of Fear That Demons Plant In Your Head To Turn Away From This Knowledge. Command The Demon Of Fear To Leave You!** Yah did not give you a spirit of fear but of a sound mind, power, and love. He will provide you with the power to cast out demons and power over serpents (**demons**) and scorpions (**Luke 10:19, 2 Timothy 1:7**). Meditate on the scriptures above if you start to feel that way.

On the other hand, some of you will not understand the spirituality of this warfare and will not grasp what is being said in the spiritual realm. However, you can ask Yah to open up your understanding and show you which demons were assigned to you and your family. I also encourage you to take the time to read this book in a quiet place with no interruptions and turn off your phone.

Do not let anyone talk you out of reading this book to do something else. Pray that Yah will release His warrior angels to fight that "**blockade spirit**," which causes people to fall asleep when reading the bible and when they are in prayer. Demons **WILL DO ANYTHING THEY CAN** to keep you from getting the knowledge that is needed for you to be free so they can kill your life. I cannot begin to tell you all of the interruptions these demons sent my way to try to keep me from writing, researching, and completing this book for publishing. **Do not be surprised** if there are all kinds of interruptions when you start reading this book to keep you from acting on suggestions that fit your situation.

There are functions of demons linked to **Principalities of Darkness** that fit every situation. This book is the first step to identifying the demons that fit the issues you are facing, and understanding the method of being delivered from them. This information will also help individuals understand why they live so hard for Yah; sanctified and filled with the Ruach **(Holy Spirit)** and the fruits of the spirit flowing in their life but still, everything they touch seems to fail. There are many scenarios explained later in detail as to what might be causing that problem.

You must remember that if your situation is not the result of willing sin, it can be linked to **"Generational Curses"** and some of the curses will not be prevented because you serve Yah. However, Yah can override, and prevent demons from interfering in individuals' lives if He wants to but Yah respect covenants so He does not interfere. Just because you are not aware of the covenants and contracts made with demons by ancestors does not stop demons from holding up Yah's will for your life. This simply means that if you are linked to generational curses, which was an ancestor that brought on tragedy to the children and grandchildren because of covenants made with demons at some point. Yah is not a liar so He lives up to His laws in scripture. His words shall not return to him void (**Isaiah 55:11**). Although it has already been ordained, and your steps are ordered by Yah? Moreover, the plans for your life can be held up due to curses and spells cast on you from your bloodline of ancestors that have done evil works against the laws of Yah.

It is written that the sins will revisit your descendants up to the third and fourth generation unless someone breaks the curse. Even if you do not understand what is going on in your life, it does not stop demons from touching your life because they remember when the covenant was made, and the ancestor that started the covenant might have been dead for fifty years but the descendants from that ancestor are still reaping the curses. Yah's people are destroyed for the lack of knowledge
(Hosea 4:6). *"My **people are destroyed for the lack of knowledge [of My law, where I reveal My will for you to be free]"**. "Because you [**the priestly nation/and chosen**] have rejected knowledge, I will also reject you from being my priest. Since you have forgotten the law of your Father Yah, I will also forget you and your children."*

Many people, including myself, thought that whatever Yah has for us nothing can stop it because Yah is the Almighty and we belong to Him. Yes, that is correct because He is all-powerful and if you belong to Him, He will protect you from some things. However, because He respects covenants some things He will allow because Yah cannot go back on His word. Always remember Satan and demons can only do what Yah allows anyway; until a family member breaks the curse. Those demons will continue until the third and fourth generations. Then as it gets closer to that third or fourth generation, those demons that have been running that family genealogy for many years do not want to leave. Therefore, they will do something to lure that third or fourth-generation family member back into the same trail of darkness to keep that generational curse going. After reading this book, if you need to **"break generational"** curses; I strongly encourage you to do so.

It is not that Yah cannot override the chaos that Satan and demons are responsible for acting out in your life. However, Yah does not interfere with covenants made with spirits of darkness, even if you are not aware of it you will reap the curses. I am a living witness; I had no idea that my life was a constant battle no matter how much I tried to do right by Yah and my people. However, Yah kept me because he knew my heart and how much I love Him. Therefore, He had mercy and grace towards me. Nevertheless, by me not knowing about the covenants that my grandmother and her husband made with demons and the things they allowed in their household until many years later. Those demons blocked many things in my life. My grandmother raised me from a age two until eight before I was returned back to my mother. So those spirits came to me at a young age because I was in her house hold and because she is my grandmother. Yah respect covenants. The words that he spoke out of his mouth cannot return to him void. Whether you are aware or not that you and your ancestors have made covenants with spirits of darkness. That will not stop demons from attacking you. If you are aware and did not know what to do that is one thing but now that you are getting knowledge through this book you need to take advantage of it break them. "Ask me how I know." My whole life of constant traumas proves it. Even when being on fire for Yah, that is why it is so important to get this knowledge I am exposing in this book.

Meaning of Covenant: An agreement by lease; deed; participation; or other legal contracts; pledge; promise; verbal agreement; commitment, vow; guarantee, or warrant.

(Isaiah 55:10-11)."*For as the rain and snow come down from heaven and do not return there without watering the earth, making it bear and sprout, providing seed to the sower, and bread to the eater,* **so will my word which goes out of my mouth. It will not return to Me void (useless, without result)**, *without accomplishing what I desire, and without succeeding in the matter for which I sent it.* Yah is saying that the laws of the weather have to do what it was made to do, all the same for his LAWS, must do as HE said they will do, without returning to HIM void because HE spoke it out of his mouth.

If you open doors for demons to come into your life by sinning against the laws of Yah, then you have entered into an agreement and covenant with the devil. Not to say that we do not fall short of sin, but our fleshly desires can tempt us. This is also a reason to ask Yah "to lead you not into temptation," and make a way of escape to avoid sinning against Him when the opportunity comes (**1Corinthians 10:13/Matthew 6:13**). This is also, why it is important to know His word to know what to do when that situation comes. The Holy Spirit will also bring back to your memory if you have read your bible, as you are to make solid decisions. However, when a person continues in that sin without repentance, demons have a right to curse individuals and cause all kinds of hardships, chaos, broken relationships, family issues, and so forth.

Nevertheless, a curse cannot happen unless there is a cause, so if you find yourself falling under the category of a curse, you must examine yourself, and watch who you keep company with (**whether family or not**). In addition, the people you let in your space may be causing the curses because they are being judged by Yah and since you are connected to them, you are being judged too (**Proverbs 22:25**). If that is the case it is mandatory to love them from a distance. Read the laws of Yah. I strongly advise you to have a relationship with Him through His Son Yahshua.

A curse cannot come without a cause (Proverbs 26:2).
Unfortunately, churches constantly speak about Yah's mercy and grace and make repetitious statements that we are saved by grace but the church does not teach in-depth about spiritual warfare or the wrath of Yah.
Isaiah 45:6-7
I am Yah, and there is no other, The one forming light and creating evil, causing peace and creating disaster; I am Yah who does all these things.
People always talk about how good YAH is and that is true. However, Yah also has another side to Him that people do not want to recognize. That is, Yah will send evil spirits to individuals who refuse to turn from sin. **For example**, suppose Yah has given a person a final answer they have been praying about. They continue to come before Him asking the same thing because they do not like His response the first time. As a result, Yah will not answer them regarding the same question, and because He knows what is in their heart in the first place to go against His answer. Yah will sometimes tell the evil spirit to go ahead and set them up for destruction or to even be killed, depending on what is being asked. Read the book of **Numbers Chapter 22** in the bible.

Satan goes before Yah, accuses individuals of unconfessed sin, and requests to go after them with curses and destruction. Guess what? Yah will grant it to him because he cannot go against His laws.

I am not talking about falling short of sin; **we all do**, and scripture says so. I am talking about willing to sin without repentance or having no sorrow which opens doors for curses, whether by Yah or Satan. Yah will approve it because Satan cannot do anything without Yah's permission. Please see the scriptures below to back up what I am conveying. Please read my book <u>**"Chosen to Break Generational Curses"**</u> when it is released. I am sharing episodes of my life that were cursed and the crazy things I encountered before I found out how to be delivered.

The curses were mostly generational and other things that I caused upon myself. I explained how demons tried to kill me from birth until adulthood, which guided me to study and research generational curses and spiritual warfare.

When I wrote this book, I learned about the breakdown of demons, which explains why I was going through the things I had gone through.

Once I learned about the functions of demons. I can freely say that most people or someone close to me has experienced the same things if not all that I have been through, but too shameful to say so. Much of it has to do with the curses that are upon so-called "black people," because of the curses that have been placed on them by the Almighty Yah. I have also released a book titled **"Who Are the True Chosen People of Yah in the Bible?"** which is listed in the bible. Understand that demons love to keep things a secret and keep them hidden, but I **wrote this book to expose them so that people can be delivered!** If you choose to stay in bondage and ignorance that is your choice, but it is no reason to stay in those circumstances after getting this knowledge. Yah says in his laws that His people are destroyed for the lack of knowledge.

I realized that I have a series of books revealing the turmoil in my life. **For example,** one of the books that I wrote, titled **"Tears for My Sisters,"** is non-fictional regarding women with real-life situations and I talk about issues I faced in life but how Yah always got me out of each situation. Whether raped, abused mentally/physically, molested, or taken for granted. The struggles of single parenting and broken relationships are some of the things that women in the Bible experienced too.

We face the same challenges today because nothing is new under the sun (**Ecclesiastics 1:9**). I talk about my own experiences and life, which is evidence of what I am explaining in this book that played a HUGE role in many situations in my life. At the time, I was writing some of my books. I did not know what I know now. Most of the information in this book I have collected through the years from experiences and research. This is also the reason why I was able to release the number of books I have in 2022 because I learned how to cast certain demons out of my life that were holding up the release of my books. Trust me when I say that these demons will hold up your progress, they will do it. If you are not aware of what is going on and holding you stagnated towards your destiny. You will know by the time you finishing reading this book.

All I know is that I struggled so hard, no matter what I did. Some would consider me a good woman because I am genuine and honest about my experiences and made it through. However, the good comes from Yah for keeping me and giving me the strength to endure and write these books and determined to get them on the shelf for individuals that need this to help them. Therefore, other women and men will relate and be blessed by reading how Yah brought me through it all. Yah has no respect of persons. When you follow Yah's laws which is His word in the bible. When you repent and exercise your faith. He can certainly do the same for you.

I know that many will read this book like a fairytale and not take it seriously. However, this book was written for those that are serious about finding out how to change constant issues in their lives. In my book "**Tears for My Sisters**." I put my business out there because I have nothing to hide and I want people to experience Yah's supernatural blessings as I did. I know that most people are open to those that can relate to their situation. Especially when they have overcome what that individual has gone through. I am now delivered from the curses that were once evident in my life. I want my readers to know that you are not crazy, and alone. You can be delivered too. This book will help those that are sick and tired and have exhausted all resources in getting help.

Most of all, I found a solution in scriptures and some so-called "**lost books**" of the Bible that were deliberately removed (**there are more than 66 books of the bible**) that helped me.

THE FOLLOWING SCRIPTURES ARE A FEW OF MANY THAT PROVE "YAH WILL SEND EVIL TO PEOPLE WHEN THEY ARE DISOBEDIENT OR REBELLIOUS"

REFERENCE SCRIPTURES:
*Numbers 22-Yah gave Balaam permission to do what he told him not to do after asking several times, then sent one of His angels to kill Balaam because he kept asking Yah the same thing after telling him no (**Balaam wanted to curse the children of Yisrael**) and there was no cause for them to be cursed because they were obeying his laws.*
*Jonah 4:17- Yah hurled a high wind toward the sea, the people became afraid, and they all called on gods that they serve. Nevertheless, the storm would not stop. Jonah was commanded to call on his God (**Yah**), but he knew that **Yah** would not listen to him because he was disobedient. Therefore, he told the crew to throw him overboard to save themselves from the storm.*
*As soon as they threw Jonah overboard, the wind stopped, and the whale swallowed Jonah. Therefore, **Yah** appointed the whale to swallow Jonah. **Your disobedience and sin can harm others around you,** whether they are a part of your sin or not. This is why you need to be careful of the people you let in your space.*

Numbers 21:16- *⁶Yah sent fiery (**burning**) serpents among the people, and they bit the people, and many Israelites died ⁷So the people came to Moses and said, "We have sinned, for we have spoken against Yah and you; pray to Yah so that He will remove the serpents from us." So Moses prayed for the people. ⁸ Then Yah said to Moses, "Make a fiery serpent [**of bronze**] and set it on a pole; and everyone who is bitten will live when he looks at it." ⁹So Moses made a serpent of bronze and put it on the pole, and it happened that if a serpent had bitten any man or woman when they looked at the bronze serpent, they lived.*

*1 Samuel 16:14 According to scripture, Yah sent an evil spirit to Saul to torment and terrify him for seeking a medium (**psychic**) to get answers. (**I recommend you to read the whole chapter**).* I cannot emphasize enough that one must be serious about their deliverance; demons are very crafty and evil entities. They only want to steal the life of humans, possess them, and kill them spiritually and physically, especially, "**Yah's chosen people**."

Suppose you are serious about being delivered from the influence of these demons running your life and are delivered from a bloodline of generational curses. In that case, you will go through a spiritual fight. In my book **"Chosen to Break Generational Curses,"** I explain **that** when a person is chosen to break "generational curses," all the troubles they will most likely go through is the fight against them with spirits of darkness because they do not want to leave that family. As you read it, and when you are ready to take on that task to be free. I suggest that you ask Father Yah to lead you into a fast, whether one day or several.

There are different ways of fasting when it comes to food. You can fast by eating fruit or nothing but liquids (**water or smoothies**), or a dry fast (**no solid food, no water**). **For beginners**, I suggest 6 am – 6 pm and escalate to 24 hours. I know that many of you are on medications, so therefore pray and ask Yah what you should do, mainly those on medication (**I do not suggest that you not eat anything at all if on medications**).

Nevertheless, let me make it clear, I am not a nutritionist or doctor, I am just making suggestions, but the decision is up to you. Read and meditate on scriptures. I encourage you to also purchase the books listed on the reference page. People can also fast from things they like to do, in exchange for spending more time in prayer, reading and studying the bible, or inspirational books, to feed their spirit and soul like this book you are currently reading. You can fast from television, from playing video games, going out with friends, social media, etc. Whatever takes up your time, you can spend that time to feed your spirit with spiritual food. You want to meditate on the scriptures of that particular thing you are praying and fasting about.

The more you engage in fasting and reading the word of Yah as well as bonding with him. The voids in your life will be filled. Once you understand the functions of demons and find out how to be delivered from them, you might start feeling motivated to cast out demons in people walking down the street. Please do not think you now have to go out and start rebuking demons in people and calling them out without being led by the **Ruach Ha Quodash**. You must be wise with the knowledge you have come to know and let the **(Holy Spirit)** lead you in spiritual warfare and to help others. Mainly focus on being delivered yourself. If you are instructed to cast demons out of someone make sure the Holy Spirit (**Ruach**) leads you.

You had also better make sure that you are clear of demons within yourself before trying to help someone else. You do not know the number of demons influencing individuals or how they entered to possess the individual, or if they are curses spoken over them when they were children that caused the demons to enter them, possess them or influence them.

Some demons are in people legally through contracts and covenants made by their ancestors and immediate family members, as in grandma, grandpa, or mommy and daddy that have come into a covenant or contract agreement. To name a few, the covenant agreement could have formed from **Sororities, Fraternities, Masonry, witchcraft, psychics, Tara Card reading, etc**. Those organizations also fall under generational curses that are detailed in my book, **"Chosen to Break Generational Curses."** Fasting will be necessary for some demons to leave but you do not always have to fast for all demons to leave. Some you have to because they are very stubborn, due to being a part of your family for generations. Once you are delivered that does not mean that the demons will never attempt to re-enter in the future. You must stay in the word of Yah, have a personal relationship with him, praise and worship Him, and always be on guard to keep these demons from re-entering with other demons worse than before. The hardships, harassment, and rejection caused in the past may appear to resurface, even if you are living holy.

Demons will try to get you to admit that they are back in your life so that they can re-enter so watch what you say, there is death and life in the power of the tongue, and those demons are just waiting for you to say something that will open a door for them to rush back in, after being delivered

Matthew 12:44.
Then it says, 'I will return to my house from which I came.' And when it arrives, it finds the place unoccupied, swept, and put in order. [45] *Then it goes and brings with it seven other spirits more wicked than itself, and they go in and make their home there. And the last condition of that man becomes worse than the first.*
This scripture is also the reason why you do not want to go casting spirits out of people without being led by the Ruach Ha Quadesh because the individual has not consciously made a decision to want to live for Yashua, repented, and confessed their sins or ancestor sins.

When you are in spiritual warfare and addressing demons. Say the following: "I know I am delivered, and you have no more power in my life, you are evicted from my life indefinite, and I command that you flee from my dwelling and atmosphere right now and every demon you have brought with you that are trying to enter back into this temple in the name of Yahshua."

Audience please note, that if you have opened doors to allow the demons to re-enter, they have a legal right to be in your life. Make sure you examine yourself carefully daily and are not guilty of willing sin against the laws of Yah.

REALITY STRIKES WHEN CASTING OUT DEMONS
I have to let you know about the backlash of this fight because I want to be one hundred percent honest with you. Some demons are very stubborn because they have been in your family for years and do not want to leave. Remember, in order for demons to operate their evil tactics; they must have a vessel to dwell. They can use anything, such as animals, objects, and people to torture. However, they prefer human beings the most because they can do more damage when they use people. They want to kill the soul of people to make them sin against Yah to be thrown into the Lake of Fire with them **(Eternal Damnation)**.

Demons are already judged and cannot be forgiven, they are guaranteed to be tossed in the lake of fire but people still have a chance to repent and follow Yah before this physical life ends. Therefore, those of you that are breaking generational curses to be free from demons operating in your family bloodline will experience the following. There may be sudden financial interferences, people acting stupid on your job concerning you, bills that come out of nowhere, family acting crazy and sometimes standoffish, and many times the children too. As these things happen, keep saying that it is all working out for my good, and my Father in heaven will supply all of my needs. I am a witness; Yah will take care of His people if you trust Him. Please also keep in mind to make sure you are not sinning somewhere in your life because it may be Yah allowing those mishaps if you need to be corrected or chastised. You know many people claim that they believe in Yah (**God**) but are not obeying his laws. So if you make that proclamation and live opposite to His laws. YOU ARE NOT PROTECTED!!!! You will experience all kinds of chaos because you are ignoring His laws as to what it says to do, if you proclaim to believe Him and state that you follow Him, you need to also follow His laws.

Hosea 4:6
Because you (**the priestly nation**) have rejected knowledge (**His laws**), I will also reject you from being My priest. Since you have forgotten the law of your Elohim, I will also forget your children.

When Satan is attacking you, he may bring things your way to irritate you, for example, things like saying good morning to people and they heard you, looked you in the face, and did not respond, not from that one person but several times that day. A neighbor playing extra loud derogatory music. Also, things may break down that will deplete your finances to get fixed, like a car, refrigerator, washing machine, television, etc. For example, you can turn on your computer. It suddenly freezes up, and then goes blank in the middle of your document (**ask me how I know**).

The computer "Breaks down for no reason" (**seems to be no reason**) especially when you have a task to do for Yah's kingdom. Part of what I am giving examples about happened to me. You will not believe the setbacks and all the things I went through to complete all my books this year. These are just a few things I am naming to give you an idea of what I am talking about. I know the examples I expressed can be stressful and make you not want to go through that process. Again, your process of deliverance casting out demons may not be the same as mine. However, I must be honest there will be a fight and some demons are so stubborn it will be a greater fight because they refuse to leave.

DO NOT GIVE UP! Continue to say the prayers and speak those scriptures over yourself that fit what you were delivered from. It is worth you and your family to be delivered. Yah is faithful and true to his laws (**word**) and promises. I cannot stress enough how much better it is if two or more people can go into a fast and pray together about their issues. The broader the covering for one another coming against these spirits, the quicker the results. When a group of people is looking out for one another and praying for one another with the understanding of spiritual warfare, the greater the deliverance (**Leviticus 26:8**). If possible, surround yourself with others that know where you are coming from and are willing to put in the work. Iron sharpens iron.

I am not saying that one person cannot do it because I am a witness that it worked for me. However, I am saying that it is even better if there are more with this plan of deliverance with you touching and agreeing. The demons behind the scene are causing the chaos to make you want to stop (**Ephesians 6:12**). **Do not let them intimidate you!** Ask Yah for his strength, and to not let you get weary in well-doing

(**Galatians 6:9**).
[9] Let us not grow weary *or* become discouraged in doing well, for at the proper time we will reap if we do not give in.

Leviticus 26:8 five of you will chase a hundred, and a hundred of you will put ten thousand to flight; your enemies will fall before you by the sword. ⁹ For I will turn toward you [**with favor and regard**] and make you fruitful and multiply you, and I will establish *and* confirm My covenant with you.

Ephesians 6:12 for our struggle is not against flesh and blood [**contending only with physical opponents**], but against the rulers, against the powers, against the world forces of this [**present**] darkness, against the spiritual *forces* of wickedness in the heavenly (**supernatural**) *places*.

CHAPTER I

The link below is a book missing from the bible because it was removed. This is where I got the *information to reference what you are about to read in chapter one. I will first explain where demons come from and then proceed with the rest.*
(http://www.esotericarchives.com/solomon/testamen.htm)

Revelations 12: 7-10
And war broke out in heaven, Michael [**the archangel**] and his angels waging war with the dragon. The dragon and his angels fought, [8] but they were not strong enough *and* did not prevail, and there was no longer a place found for them in heaven. [9] The great dragon (**Satan**) was thrown down. The age-old serpent is called the devil, and Satan *continually* deceives *and* seduces the entire world; he was thrown down to the earth, and his angels were thrown down with him.

[10] Then I heard a loud voice in heaven, saying. Now the salvation, and the power, and the kingdom (**dominion, reign**) of our Yah; and the authority of His son Yahshua has come for the accuser of our [**believing**] brothers and sisters. He was thrown down [**at last**], he who accuses (**the chosen people of Yah**) and keeps bringing charges [**of sinful behavior**] against them before Yah, day and night. As scripture says, we need to examine ourselves daily. This is the reason for keeping a submissive will to repent and ask for forgiveness of sins that we are unaware of whether by deed or thought, unconsciously or consciously. But we all fall short of something every day.

*"Demons are on earth because of two reasons; the first reason is that Satan's angels were thrown out of heaven with him and as a result, their nature became evil like Satan. The second reason is that angels from the third heavens (**Yah's angels**) desired the daughters of men (**on earth**), they left heaven to come to the earth, to take the daughters of men as wives."* **Please see the scriptures below to back up this statement.**

Genesis 6:1-7

Now it happened when men began to multiply on the face of the land. So daughters were born to them, that the sons of Yah (**angels in heaven**) saw that the daughters of men on earth were beautiful *and* desirable. Therefore they took them as wives for themselves, whomever they chose *and* desired. Then Yah said, "My Spirit shall not strive *and* remain with man forever, because he is indeed flesh [**sinful, corrupt—given over to sensual appetites**]; nevertheless, his days shall be a hundred and twenty years (**time frame given to repent**)."

There were Nephilim (**men of stature, notorious men**) on the earth in those days—and afterward—when the sons of Yah took the daughters of men as wives, the daughters gave birth to their *children*. They became mighty men who became old. Men of renown (**great reputation and fame**). Yah saw that man's wickedness (**depravity**) was great on the earth and that every imagination and intent of the thoughts of their heart was only evil continually.

Yah regretted that He made humankind on the earth, and He was [**deeply**] grieved in His heart. So Yah said, "I will destroy (**annihilate**) mankind whom I have created from the surface of the earth—not only man but the animals and the crawling things and the birds of the air—because it [**deeply**] grieves Me [**to see mankind's sin**] *and* I regret that I have made them (**Genesis 6:6-7**)."

I know that some of you may say that is a contradiction according to the book of **Jude 1:6.** However, the angels that are spoken of in Jude have committed something worse. Please see the breakdown of the scripture below for your understanding.

*Angels who did not keep their designated place of power (**in the heavens**), but abandoned their proper dwelling place, Yah has kept in eternal chains under [**the thick gloom of utter**] in darkness, waiting for the judgment of the great day.*

*Just as Sodom & Gomorrah and the adjacent cities (**surrounding cities**) did. Sodom & Gomorrah were full of homosexuality. Those angels indulged in gross immoral freedom, unnatural vice, and sensual perversity (**the angels spoken of in Jude had sex with men*** *instead of women). Homosexuality is an abomination to Yah (Leviticus 18:22). Therefore, the angels in a dwelling place of punishment locked in chains are held there until the day of judgment, and then they will be cast into the lake of fire with the others.* **Homosexuality is a very strong unclean spirit. Yah considers this an unnatural act against human nature to procreate.**

Romans 1:27: *In the same way also the men turned away from the natural function of the woman and were consumed with their desire towards one another, men with men committing shameful acts and in return receiving in their bodies the inevitable and appropriate penalty for their wrongdoing.*
Yah made Solomon (**King David's son**) the wisest man in the world to be a judge for Israel. People came to him to get issues resolved (**like a judge**).

The Book of Solomon (**one of the books removed from the bible**). This particular section below was removed.

Yah gave Solomon authority over demons too. Solomon would command them to convey (say) to him what they do and why. Then he would make them do something they hate to do. It was recorded in "**The Book of Solomon**" that there was an old man and his only son who went before Solomon to resolve an issue. Solomon began talking to the demons. Please note, it is **<u>NOT</u>** advised to talk to demons unless you are trying to deliver someone from a spirit and you command it to tell you what is its name to call it out or ask how and when did it enter the individual. Solomon was authorized to have conversations with demons. Then, the young man's father (**old man**) came to Solomon for advice to avenge on his behalf against his son. The old man stated that his son abused him by pulling his hair out and violently threatening to kill him. Solomon felt pity for the old man and made his son apologize to him.

However, the son denied it, and at the same time apologized out of respect; Solomon then told the father of the boy to forgive his son as well. Scripture says that **we are to honor our parents (Leviticus 19:3),** so I guess that is why the son did not speak up for himself (**not saying that what his father did was right**).

Ephesians 6:2

HONOR [**esteem, value as precious**] YOUR FATHER AND YOUR MOTHER [**and be respectful to them**]—this is the first commandment with a promise. If anyone breaks this law, they are in violation and will face Yah's judgment. Not to say that you are to submit to the wrongdoing of your parents, nevertheless, that is probably the reason the young man apologized knowing his father was lying (**out of respect**). The father refused and wanted his son killed anyway. This goes to show from the beginning of time, people had evil hearts and did not love their children, as they should.

Just before Solomon was about to give the man what he wished for, **a demon by the name of Ornias (that consumes people's finances and nutrients from the body)** was laughing. Solomon paused from the process and became angry that the demon was laughing in his presence and called the devil to ask why he was laughing. The demon replied that he was not laughing at him; he was laughing at what was about to happen. The scripture described the boy's father as "ill-starred"(**nothing fruitful in his life**). The scripture also referenced him as wretched, **meaning worthless, inadequate, and inferior.**

The demon continued to explain to Solomon that the old man's son would have died a premature death within three days. Therefore, his father would have gotten away with it **(there is proof that death can be premature according to the bible in Ecclesiastics 7:17), if it is Yah's will to let it happen.** "In other words, the father wanted his son dead because he wanted nothing to do with him **(the book of Solomon does not say why).** Solomon would have killed him before his time." Yah did not allow it because it would not have been a justifiable death. The young boy's father would have been satisfied that he had gotten Solomon to kill him without having to face the punishment for the murder of his son. Solomon asked the demon **"was that true**," and the demon replied, **"Yes."**

Nevertheless, Solomon made the older man and his son return and ordered them to make peace with each other, and then he gave them food. Solomon also told the boy's father to bring his son back to check on him in three days. They saluted Solomon and went on their way.

Solomon demanded the demon named **Ornias** to tell him how did he know that, and he said to Solomon' "We demons ascend into the firmament (**sky**) of heaven and fly about among the stars. They hear the sentences which go forth upon the souls of men **(prayers and conversations),** and instantly we come **(to act on negative words spoken out of their mouths and/or fight against their prayers).** This is the reason why I constantly tell people to watch what they say because there is **"Death and Life"** in the tongue. You speak positive things over yourself and someone else. When you speak negative and death, <u>**demons are waiting to act on it**</u> you just read it as proof according to what the demon said to Solomon. Those that curse others out of their mouth by speaking negative things. Be careful what you say and it must be justified.

Because it is a dangerous thing to curse someone (**Yah's people**) or something that Yah has blessed. Whether it is by mouth, witchcraft, spells, etc. **Numbers 23:8,** "How shall I curse those whom Yah has not cursed? On the other hand, how can I [**violently**] denounce those Yah has not denounced? **Numbers 23:20,** "Behold, I have received *His command* to bless [**Israel**]. He has blessed me, and I cannot reverse it. Maybe this could also be the reason some of you are in turmoil for cursing someone that was blessed, or should I say tried to, however, even if you tried to and it was not justified. Yah will allow that curse to boomerang back to you. I am not talking about using cuss words (**profanity**), although that can also play a part in it. **For example,** those that use the cuss word "Mother F_cker," you are cursing your mother each time it is said. The word "F_ck" is the name of a demon, it is under the list with the names of demons and their evil functions in this book. Yah says, those that curse individuals that belong to Him, He will curse the one doing the cursing. Those that bless that individual, Yah will bless them.

Definition of a curse: a solemn utterance intended to invoke a supernatural power to inflict harm or punishment on someone or something. **For example,** one might curse someone out of jealousy and envy. I remember a woman that I met at a retreat and some years later we crossed paths and exchanged phone numbers. She was telling me how she always wanted to open up a flower shop at a particular location.

She said that the spot was vacant for a long time and one day she drove by it and saw that someone rented the location and opened a flower shop. She said that she was so jealous that she looked at the shop and said, "She hopes the business fails and shut down." She said within six months to a year the shop shut down." I cannot remember the exact number but it was a short period. She continued to say that she felt bad about it and she said before she came to the truth about the laws of Yah in the bible. Although she was aware of the truth of the scriptures later, the curse she spoke over someone else's business came back to her. She had forgotten what she did, so she came to Yah, and asked for forgiveness. She lost a thriving business she had, and became sick, and had to let the business go. Therefore, the curse she spoke over someone else came back full circle along with sickness.

Getting back to the confessions that the demon was telling Solomon. The demon continues speaking to Solomon; the demons stated whether by force to influence, or by fire, sword, or some accident, we prevail in our acts of destruction. "If a man does not die by some untimely disaster or by violence **(Ecclesiastics 7:17),** then we demons change ourselves to appear to men like angels of light **and to be worshipped in human nature."** Angels of light meaning to come to people as friendly with a smile. They are familiar with your desires and prayers. Therefore, they will transform themselves into whatever they desire **as an angel of light**. So be aware!

For example: say you desire a husband or wife. Demons hear your conversations and prayers and the type of husband or wife that you describe that you want. They will come as an angel of light to be just what you prayed for. The conversation will be awesome, you have much in common they look like what you want and desire, etc.

This is why I say always include Yah in everything. It is recommended to always say, "If it is Yah's will." (**James 4:15**) Instead you ought to say, "If Yah will, we will do this and we will do that." You also need to test the spirit because Satan and demons always come with some truth mixed with lies as wolves in sheep's clothing. If you do not test the spirits to see if they are real, as well as seek Yah's approval. Once you get married all hell breaks loose. This is why part of our daily prayer should be that Yah delivers us from all evil, and leads us **NOT** into temptation. In addition, whatever you desire and pray for, you should end it with, if it is Yah's will.

Regarding the true names of Yah and Yahshua, some individuals may not know the names yet so pray and ask Yah if they know the truth. Some of you that are reading this book might not have known the true names of the almighty Yah and his son Yahshua until you read this book. I have learned throughout life that we have our thoughts and desires for our life but sometimes they are not Yah's desire for our life (**Isaiah 55:8-9**). That is why I say, first pray, and then end your prayers with **"if it is Yah's will."** Satan and demons know scripture too but are not obeying it. You need to always test the spirit; even Satan knows how to quote scriptures. (**1 John 4:1-6**)

DO NOT LET THEM TRICK YOU BECAUSE THEY QUOTE SCRIPTURE! If there is no fruit then you know what is real.
Isaiah 55:8-9
"For My thoughts are not your thoughts, nor are your ways My ways," declares Yah. "For as the heavens are higher than the earth, so are My ways higher than your ways and My thoughts higher than your thoughts.

1 John 4:1-9
Beloved, do not believe every spirit, but test the spirits to see whether they are from Yah, for many false prophets have gone out into the world. ² By this you know the Spirit of Yah: every spirit that confesses that Yahshua the Messiyah has come in the flesh is from Yah, ³ and every spirit that does not confess Yahshua is not from Yah. This is the spirit of the antichrist, which you heard was coming and now is in the world already. ⁴ Little children, you are from Yah and have overcome them, for he who is in you is greater than he who is in the world. ⁵ They are from the world;

therefore, they speak from the world, and the world listens to them. [6] We are from Yah. Whoever knows Yah listens to us; whoever is not from Yah does not listen to us. By this, we know the Spirit of truth and the spirit of error.

Solomon then asked the evil spirit, "how do you ascend in heaven being demons *and amidst the stars and holy angels intermingle.*" The demon responds "just as things are rewarded in heaven and on earth (*are fulfilled*), all types." **There are principalities, authorities, and world rulers, and we demons fly about in the air (Ephesians 6:12).** "We hear the voices of the heavenly beings and survey to query (**demand**), a demon to collect data for the analysis and all the powers."

The response that demon explained to Solomon lets me know that demons have access to go up to the third heavens where Yah, Yahshua, and the angels of Yah dwell. They hear the conversations discussed regarding the people of Yah. They can hear how Yah wants to bless His people and His purpose for them while on this Earth. The demon comes back with the report to share with other demons to do everything they can to throw individuals off track from the blessings and the will of Yah for their life. They will try to get you to sin against the laws of Yah so that they have a right to block it. When we sin against the laws of Yah, many times whatever Yah's blessing was for you is lost once a person yields to sin.

Especially dealing with demonic things, like **witchcraft, Tara Card reading, Ouji Board game playing, sexual sin etc.** This is why we must have a prayer life and a relationship with Yah. Admonish one another, pray for one another, and fight spiritual warfare together. As well, as study the scriptures for ourselves so that we will not sin against Yah's laws and sin against Him.

Matthew 16:19
*whatever you bind [**forbid, declare to be improper and unlawful**] on earth [g]will have [**already**] been bound in heaven, and whatever you loosed [**permit, maintain lawful**] on the ground [h]will have [**already**] been loosed in heaven.*"

Demons are very real, they are unseen evil spirits, but some of them were giants that once walked the earth, their human nature carried out evil deeds because that was their demeanor when they were in the flesh. Nevertheless, when they died, the flesh went back to the ground as dirt. However, the spirit lives on, and they became evil spirits that influence people to do evil and possess them. They like to use a human being to dwell in to either influence, oppress, suppress or possess to carry out their despicable tactics."

There were Nephilim (**men of stature, notorious men**) on the earth in those days—and afterward—when the sons of Yah lived with the daughters of men, and they gave birth to their children. These were the mighty men who were of old, men of renown *(great reputation, fame)* **because of the babies conceived through the daughters of men and the angels of Yah.** They were half human and half supernatural and became demons when the natural man died, but the spirit lives on to roam the earth and influence evil upon men.

Again, as mentioned before. **Please Note….Yah DOES NOT** want us to carry on conversations with demons. He gave Solomon that privilege for reasons back then. The only time that may be necessary to do this is if you are delivering someone that is possessed by demons and you command that the demon tell you the name of it. If you do not recognize it from any of the names in this book. **Below are *three scriptures*** that prove the conversations Solomon had with the demons about being able to go in and out of the third heavens of Yah.

When he asked, "how are they able to ascend in the heavens being demons, and amidst intermingle with the holy angels." The answer is also shown in the scriptures below.

Yah's approval to allow Satan to test Job's faith (Job 1:6-7).
The day came to be when the sons (**angels**) of Yah came to present themselves before Yah, and Satan (**the accuser**) came among them (**in the third heavens**).

Mathew 16: 18-19: [18] And I say that you are [d]Peter. On this [e]rock, I will build My assembly, and the [f]gates of Hades (**death**) will not overpower it [**by preventing the resurrection of Yahshua**]. [19] I will give you the keys (**authority**) of the kingdom of heaven; and *whatever you bind [forbid, declare to be improper and unlawful] on earth [g]will have [already] been bound in heaven, and whatever you loosed [permit, maintain lawful] on the ground [h]will have [already] been loosed in heaven."*

Therefore, **this scripture shows the evil one can also go to the third heavens** and hear what is said about people on earth; they also hear the prayers going up to the heavens. Because **they can hear what conversations are discussed and people on earth,** Satan goes before Yah for permission to attack Yah's people if they are willfully sinning. Remember the quote below when the demon said to Solomon. "He answered, just as things are rewarded in heaven and on earth (**are fulfilled**), all types." There are principalities, authorities, and world rulers, we demons fly about in the air. What you just read above is the following scriptures: **whatever you bind [forbid, declare to be improper and unlawful] on earth [g]will have [already] been bound in heaven, and whatever you loosed [permit, maintain lawful] on the ground [h]will have [already] been loosed in heaven."**

Ephesians 6:12 for our struggle is not against flesh and blood [**contending only with physical opponents**], but against the rulers, against the powers, against the world forces of this [**present**] darkness, against the spiritual forces of wickedness in the heavenly (**supernatural**) places. This is the reason it is important to know Yah's laws because you will know what you are coming against in the spiritual world.

Below are *three scriptures that back up the conversation Solomon had with that demon:*

1.) (Job 1:6-7 Yah's approval to Satan to test job faith)
 And the day came to be when the sons (**angels**) of Yah came to present themselves before Yah, and Satan (**devil**) came among them (**in the third heavens**). Therefore, **this scripture shows that the evil one can also go to the third heavens** and hear what is said about people on earth; they also hear the prayers going up to the

heavens. Because **they can hear what conversations are discussed about the people on earth,** Satan goes before Yah for permission to attack Yah's people if they are willfully sinning.

Job's Testing :

*Now there was a day when the sons of Yah (**angels**) came to present themselves before Yah, and Satan (**adversary, accuser**) also came among them. ⁷Yah said to Satan, "From where have you come?" Then Satan answered Yah, "From roaming around on the earth and from walking around on it." ⁸ Yah said to Satan, "Have you considered and reflected on My servant Job? For there is none like him on the earth, a blameless and upright man, one who fears Yah [**with reverence**] and abstains from and turns away from evil [**because he honors Yah**]."*

*Then Satan answered the Yah, "Does Job fear Yah for nothing? ¹⁰ Have You not put a hedge [**of protection**] around him and his house and all that he has, on every side? You have blessed the work of his hands [**and conferred prosperity and happiness upon him**], and his possessions have increased in the land. ¹¹ But put forth Your hand now and touch (**destroy**) all that he has, and he will surely curse You to Your face." ¹² Then Yah said to Satan, "Behold, all that Job has is in your power, only do not put your hand on the man himself." So Satan departed from the presence of Yah.*

Yah will grant Satan's wish to afflict them because he cannot go against his rules (**word/laws**). Satan (**the accuser**) and all demons know this, and that is why they want to deceive Yah's people to sin against Him. If demons are successful in getting individuals to sin willfully and not repent of it. They can legally attack them. When people are out of the will of Yah, they are unprotected. This is why we are to examine ourselves daily and judge ourselves so that Yah will not have to judge us because we have judged ourselves (**we must die daily to ourselves**).

2.) (Mathew 18:18); indeed, I say to you, whatever you bind on earth shall be bound in heaven, and whatever you loose on earth shall be loosed in heaven.

3.) (Ephesians 6:12); we do not wrestle against flesh and blood, but principalities, against authorities, against the world rulers of all the darkness of this age, against spiritual matters of wickedness in the heavenly. *In addition, Yah may brag about one of his servants and request that Satan tries them **(Yah knows how much each person can endure, so he tells Satan what his limitations are if he allows him to afflict the individual)**.*

*This scripture can be referenced in the book of **Job 1: 7-8.***
*Although Yah knew Job's heart and his outcome, Job feared the same things that Yah allowed Satan to attack him with. I never noticed until someone brought it to my attention, that Job had a fear that all the tragedies that happened to him had come to pass. **Yah has not given us a spirit of fear, but of love, power, and a sound mind;** fear is an evil spirit; this spirit always tries to impose on people, especially Yah's people, while being accompanied by other evil spirits to doubt Yah.*

*(**Job 3:25-26**); (**"for that which I greatly feared has come upon me, and that which I dreaded has overtaken me."** (26) "I have not been at ease, nor have I been undisturbed nor been at rest, yet trouble comes!"*

HOROSCOPE SIGNS ARE DEMONIC, AND SO ARE OLD WIVES' TALES A.K.A "OMENS"

THE FOLLOWING PROVES THAT ZODIAC SIGNS ARE NAMES OF DEMONS

Solomon was having a conversation with demons to find out what evil they do; Solomon's conversation with these demons reveals evidence that the names and signs of horoscopes are evil. The names of zodiac signs/horoscopes are actual demons. There is **danger in participating in horoscopes** and **zodiac signs**.

According to this missing book, this demon calls itself the thirty-six elements. She said to Solomon, **"we are many in one."** "The *thirty-six elements world ruler of darkness, we present ourselves before you like the other spirits, from ram (**Aries**), and bull (**Taurus**), from both twin (**Gemini**), and crab (**Cancer**), lion (**Leo**) and*

*virgin (**Virgo**), scales (**Libra**), and (**Scorpio**) archer, (**Sagittarius**)
goat-horned, (**Capricorn**) water-pourer, (**Aquarius**), and
fish (**Pisces**)."*

*When people identify themselves with zodiac names, they are connecting themselves to demons. Think about it, why would someone want to call him or herself **"cancer"** anyway? Each one of these demons has an evil task to do. When you identify yourself with it, you open doors for those demons to come in and take over your life, whether it be your **health, finances, causing family dysfunctions, etc**.*

*It does not matter how deep and spiritually you are in Yah. If you engage in things like this, demons are at your doorstep causing all kinds of chaos, Yah will allow it because His word will not return to Him void. He respects covenants, and when one makes a covenant with demons, whether they know it or not, they are guilty of it, and Yah's hand of safety will not protect them. Some might say, "But what if you did not know?" That is why it is imperative to study the scriptures for yourself and know what you are to do, according to Yah's word, and be upright before Yah to have his protection. Scripture says, "My people are destroyed for lack of knowledge [**of My law, where I reveal my will**]" (Hosea 4:6).*

Yah warns us in his word to stay away from such evil participation. When you engage in anything that comes against the word of Yah. Demons have a right to torture you and carry out their ill will because you have erased the safety net of Yah from you and your family when you engage in anything that Yah said not to do. Just because you are not aware of it or choose to ignore it does not mean that the ramifications will not occur; the following scriptures below are proof. I encourage you to look them up and read them for yourself.

Isaiah 8:19-22 (Consulting Mediums)
Leviticus 19:31 (Do not turn to psychics who pretend to talk to the dead)
Deuteronomy 4:1-4 (Yah destroyed someone for participating in the worship of Baal)

Ezekiel 13:20-22 (Yah explains that he is against magic and pagan practices)
Nahum 3:4-6. (Yah speaks about the punishment he will place on this person for sorcery practices)

*Yah gave Solomon the authority to carry out judgments; He also gave him the power to summons demons (**not to do evil but command**) and tell them what to do; Solomon commanded them to do work like help build things for the kingdom that they hated, then he sends them away. Moreover, Solomon continues to speak with the*

demons; the demon explained to Solomon how they fly about in the air.

*They hear the voices of the heavenly beings (**done and said in heaven**) and study all the powers. "We **lose strength and fall** off like leaves from trees." Nevertheless, men imagine that the stars are falling from heaven (**the demon is talking about falling stars**). They fall because of their weakness and have nowhere or anything or no one to dwell in. The demon said to Solomon, "we fall like lightings in the depth of night suddenly." Having nobody to reside in, they wander in dry places and rest not (**Matthew 12:43**). **Therefore, we should rejoice when we see falling stars.*** This is also why we have to be mindful of nursery rhymes that are connected to demonic things that are taught to our children. Not saying that the people who wrote the nursery rhymes are into some kind of witchcraft or anything, but unknowingly wrote something that seems innocent and is harmful in the spiritual realm. This is an excellent example of how Satan can use you and you do not know it with things that seem innocent. Like twinkle-twinkle little star, How I wonder what you are? Reciting that rhyme can invite demons into their little nursery to show them what and who they are. It may seem far-fetched, but it is real. Demons try to befriend children with imaginary people as their friends to embrace them as a dwelling place. They may appear in their stuffed animals and dolls to scare them or make noises in their closets to make them afraid, and then the spirit of fear is invited in.

Also, the scripture of Matthew 12:43 backs up this conversation, to know that when spirits have nowhere to go. They get weak and have no rest; according to what this demon tells Solomon, they fall away because they have no place to dwell. When demons influence someone we must remember that it is not the person but the demon spirit speaking through a person. Instead of coming against the person who fuels the demon by giving it the energy to stay active, rebuke it by speaking Yah's word against the spirit. **Ephesians 6:12 says** we do not wrestle against flesh and blood, but principalities, against authorities, against the world-rulers of the darkness of this age, against spiritual matters of wickedness in the heavenly places.

The Thirty-Six Elements: Thirty-Six spirits, their heads shapeless like dogs, they were human in form, with faces of asses (**donkey**), faces of oxen, and faces of birds.

These demons are world rulers of darkness in this world; each one has its name and is responsible for its evil throughout the world we dwell in.
http://esotericarchives.com/solomon/testamen.htm

The following are the names of Demons & Their Evil Functions

1.) **The first is Raux**; he is the first demon from the zodiacal circle (*called ram/Aries*); he causes the **heads of men to be idle (*vain, idle chatter, empty pleasure*)**

2.) **The second is Barsafael,** and he causes those who are subject to his hour to feel **the pain of a migraine.**

3.) **The third is Arotosael**, responsible for harming **the eyes** and grievously injuring them

4.) **The fifth is Iudal,** which causes the **ears to be deaf**

5.) **The sixth is Sphendonael,** whose duties are to **cause tumors of the parotid gland, inflammations of the tonsils**, and tetanic recurvation

6.) **The seventh Sphandor,** responsible for weakening the strength of the shoulders and causing them to tremble; **paralyzes the nerves of the hands, breaks, and bruises the bones of the neck**, as well as sucks out the marrow

7.) **The eighth is Belbel;** he distorts the hearts and minds of men

8.) **The ninth is Kurtael;** this spirit sends **colics (abdominal pain or obstruction in the intestinal)** in the bowel and induces pain **(torment babies)**

9.) **The tenth is Metahiax**, employed to cause reins to ache (*the region of the kidneys: LOINS*)

10.) **The eleventh is Katanikotael**, who causes strife, wrongs in men's homes, and sends them hard temper (*rage, uncontrolled anger, violent wrath*)

11.) **The twelfth is Saphathorael,** who inspire partisanship (*meaning one exhibiting blind, prejudiced, and unreasoning allegiance*) in men and delight in causing them to stumble

12.) **The thirteenth is Bobel,** who causes nervous illness by assaults **a: violent physical or verbal attack; b: a military attack usually involving direct combat with enemy forces; 2a: a threat or attempt to inflict offensive physical contact or bodily harm on a person** (*as by lifting a fist in a threatening manner*) that puts the person in immediate danger of or in the apprehension of such damage or contact

13.) **The fourteenth is Kumeatel,** which inflicts shivering fits and coma (*a state of mental and motor inactivity with partial or total insensibility*)

14.) **The fifteenth is Roeled, which** causes cold and frost and pain in the stomach

15.) **The sixteenth is Atrax;** this evil demon inflicts upon men fevers, irremediable and harm

16.) **The seventeenth is Ieropael;** this demon sits on the stomach of men and causes convulsions in the bath and the road; wherever this demon is found, or when he finds a man to throw him down

17.)**The eighteenth is Buldumech, which** separates wives from husbands and brings about a grudge between them.
18.)**The nineteenth is Naoth,** who sits on the knees of men
19.)**The twentieth is Mardero, who** sends an incurable fever
20.)**The twenty-first is Alath, which** causes coughing and hard breathing in children
21.)**The twenty-third is Nefthada,** which causes the reins to ache. He brings about dysury (***painful discharge of urine***), and STD.
22.)**The twenty-fourth is Akton,** which causes ribs and limbic muscles to ache
23.)**The twenty-fifth is Anatreth**; this demon renders burnings and fevers into the entrails (*internal parts*)
24.)**The twenty-sixth is Enenuth, who** steals the minds of men and changes their hearts, and makes a man toothless
25.)**The twenty-seventh is Pheth, which** causes men to consumptive (***copious discharge of blood from the blood vessels***)
26.)**The twenty-eight is Harpax,** which causes sleeplessness in people (***insomnia***)
27.)**The twenty-ninth is Anoster, which** causes uterine mania and pains in the bladder
28.)**The thirtieth is Alleborith, which** causes one that eats fish from a bone to swallow a bone to choke them to death
29.)**The thirty-first is Hephesimireth,** which causes lingering disease
30.)**The thirty-second is Ichthion; which** causes paralyze muscles and contuse (***injury to tissue usually without laceration: BRUISE***); 1: to tear or rend roughly: wound jaggedly; 2: to cause sharp mental or emotional pain to DISTRESS
31.)**The thirty-third is Agchonion**; this spirit lies in swaddling clothes and in the precipice (*narrow strips of cloth (like a mummy) wrapped around an infant to restrict movement*). **I believe this spirit also causes SIDS**
32.)**The thirty-fourth is Authothith,** which causes grudges and fighting
33.)**The thirty-fifth is Phthenoth, who** casts an evil eye on every man

34.)**The thirty-six is Bianakith, who** has a grudge against the body, lays waste houses, causes flesh to decay, and everything else similar. **There were only 34 elements listed; the fourth and the twenty-second demon were not recorded.**

RECOGNIZING OMENS
BETTER KNOWN AS "OLD WIVES TALES"

Interpreting omens is somewhat the same as divination (**seeking knowledge of the future or the unknown**). When one participates with omens, they are co-conspirators to their demise. When one engages in this wickedness, one opens themselves to demons. The plan that Yah had for their life will be re-routed with years of hardship, poverty, setbacks, financial loss, promotions, marriage ending in divorce, having nothing, losing everything due to the plan of their life, and being high-jacked by evil spirits of darkness. When one participates in any divination, there are consequences to face.

Superstitions are considered "Omens"
Dictionary Definition of Omen: *an occurrence or phenomenon believed to portend a future event: AUGURY;* ***Definition of AUGURYL:*** divination from auspices or omens; also: an instance of this 2: OMEN, PORTENT

I guess Stevie Wonder was on to some truth when he made the song **"Superstition."** I copied and paste a small verse of the song to prove my point, which is the following.

Very superstitious, writing's on the wall, ladders bout' to fall, Thirteen-month-old baby, broke the lookin' glass seven years of bad luck, The good things in your past are when you believe in things that you don't understand, then you suffer, superstition ain't the way

Examples of Omens That People Believe in and Practice:

1. If a child looks between a woman's legs-indicates	the woman is pregnant
2. Dreaming of fish	someone is pregnant
3. The palm of someone's hand itching	money coming to them
4. Ear itching	someone is talking about them
5. Nose itching	someone is going to visit them
6. Two people split the pole	bad luck will come to them
7. A full moon	good for fertilization
8. Eye is jumping	someone is supposed to visit
9. Someone steps on the crack of a sidewalk	the back of that person's mother will break
10. When a mirror is broken	the person that broke it is supposed to get seven years of bad luck
11. According to pregnancy	Carrying a baby high means, you are having a boy while carrying low means it is a girl.
12. If two or more people say something at the same time	They knock on the table and say, "knock on wood."
13. Tie a ring on a string and hang it over your belly	if it swings in a circular motion, you could be having a girl, but if it's swinging side to side, it means you're having a boy

If you are guilty of these sins, it is not too late to **REPENT** Because you have been taught the truth. Ask Yah to forgive you for identifying yourself with these demonic practices and repent; renounce, denounce, and reject anything that has to do with it in the name of Yahshua. If you have ever visited any psychic, engaged in palm reading, tarot card reading, applied horoscopes to yourself, or joined organizations like **Sororities' Fraternities**, and

Masons/Eastern Star, you need to repent and ask Yah for forgiveness.

If you are practicing **Omens** and applying **Horoscopes** to yourself by reading, proclaiming, and believing them. You have dangerously opened yourself up to a portal for demonic forces to set your life up for failure and not just you, but your descendants for up to four generations. If someone does not break the covenant, your children, grandchildren, and great-grandchildren that have not been born yet will be affected by it **(Exodus 34:7). I HAVE TO MAKE THIS KNOWN.** Some of you that are practicing some of these things may say well I am doing this or that and my life is fine. For right now, because Satan is deceiving you and manipulating you into thinking your life is fine. In due time, you will see that it is not.

I hope that you will find out before you close your eyes and leave this planet for good or before it is too late, otherwise, you will be in for a rude awakening when you see your **"MAKER."** Your life seems grand because Satan already using you to join him in the lake of fire so he and his agents (**other demons and people that worship him**) will not bother you much. Satan and demons are constantly after those individuals that are trying to live a righteous life for Yah but are not aware that they are tied to generational curses from covenants and contracts made by ancestors, or things they have engaged in at some point, not knowing that it was tied to the dark world. **For example**, getting their palms read or playfully, taking someone's hand, or their own hand, and making something up about their life. There was a covenant made with demons to redirect your pathway of life that Yah intended for you to have on this earth in your journey for your call. Satan and demons hijacked the plans that Yah had for your life journey, of blessings.

Therefore, you can be a follower of Yahshua's teaching and live to please Yah the best way you can and the breakthrough will come but suddenly shuts down because demons remember the covenant and contracts made with them. Until it is broken, they will continue to torture that individual. Meanwhile, they are also hoping that you will never find out so that you can eventually turn your back on Yah and say to Him that His word is not real and that He must not be real either to allow those things to continue to happen. Demons will make it look like Yah is playing games with them. Yah, is not a man that He should lie (**Numbers 23:19**). Because they keep trusting in Him and believing Him for breakthroughs, the breakthroughs will come, but they will shut down quickly because those demons interfered knowing that your ancestors, and/or yourself have made covenants or contracts with demons and the portal was connected to enter your life and hold up the blessings that Yah want you to have. Remember Yah respects covenants.

Numbers 23:19
"Yah is not a man, that He should lie, nor a son of man, that He should repent. Has He said, and will He not do it?
or has He spoken and will He not make it good *and* fulfill it?

Now that you know the truth, what will you do? Do not make the mistake of blaming Yah. Go to Yah in prayer; ask Him to bring back your memory of things that you have engaged in which made a covenant with demons according to what you have learned in this book. Also, acknowledge and ask for forgiveness on behalf of your ancestors that have made covenants and contracts with Satan and demons. If you see a pattern of things in your family that identify with demons in the list of demons and their evil functions. That is a good way to start your cleaning to get rid of these demons in you and your family life. If you see a pattern of never getting ahead, never finishing what you started, **always being broke**, **and cannot keep a job**, **all kinds of sicknesses that run through the family for generations,** difficulty to keep a relationship, and many other things. It is because of the principalities of darkness that is in a legal contract and covenant due to some covenant agreement of evil. Someone in the family caused it, or you did it to yourself by way of an organization and evil practices, subscribing to Omens, or living outside of the laws of Yah.

Definition of Witchcraft: a system of oppression, set up by evil corrupt people who practice witchcraft that causes people to have hardship, sickness, setbacks, strife amongst the family, premature deaths, orchestrated witches, warlocks, and wizards *(warlocks and wizards are male witches)*. An altar is where evil words and spells of witchcraft speak against an individual or the entire family.

WITCHES SAY THINGS LIKE THIS AT EVIL ALTERS
*"We all agree that we do not want Jane Doe/John Doe to prosper; we speak everything they put their hands to will fail (**they use the person's specific name**).We agree that the curse will run the course of blockage (**for several years**) of their life. By this time, they will lose all faith in Yah and turn their back on Yah. We speak about the illness of cancer set in their body at the age of twenty-five and that they die a premature death at the age of twenty-six.*

There is proof in scripture that people can die before their time and YAH will allow it if they continue to be wicked and sin against His laws and are overly wicked. **See the scripture below.**

Ecclesiastes 7:17: Do not be excessively *or* willfully wicked and do not be a fool. **Why should you die before your time?** [18] It is good that you take hold of one thing (**righteousness**) and also not let go of the other (**wisdom**); for the one who fears *and* worships Yah [**with awe-filled reverence**] will come forth with both of them. These spirits of darkness **ARE REAL** and hate people; they will use witches (**female witch**), warlocks (**male witch**), wizards (**male witch**), and sorcery to help get their evil works done. Most of all, the chosen people of Yah are the most targeted. They initiate a person's life to derail Yah's original plans for their lives. These spirits are agents of Satan and Satan himself who speak against people because of a covenant made with them. They can do evil through projections initiated by wicked spirits. The spirit of rejection follows them no matter where they go and will influence anyone and situations to reject them.

EXAMPLES OF GENERATIONAL CURSES FROM SOMEONE ENGAGING IN WICKEDNESS

Example One: Great-grandma might have died from breast cancer; her daughter died from breast cancer; the granddaughter died from breast cancer; the great-great-grand-daughter, many times all within the same age range.

Example Two: Everyone in your immediate family ends up with some kind of sickness or crippling condition and collects disability by age forty.

Example Three: All the girls in the family end up being teenage moms or having babies out of wedlock and never marrying for generations and generations until someone recognizes this and breaks the cycle.

EXAMPLES OF THE SPIRIT OF REJECTION WORKING IN INDIVIDUALS' LIVES

Example One: John Doe signed up to attend a trade school; he has won a scholarship to pay for his tuition along with a student loan. After the full tuition was covered. The portion leftover becomes a refund to John Doe. All of his classmates and other students are talking about how they received their refund and spent it. Nevertheless, when it came time for John Doe to get his refund, suddenly a new policy was enforced to send the refund back to the lender to help pay off the loan portion of his tuition without his consent. Moreover, immediately after he finished paying off his portion of the loan. The **"trade school"** was mishandling money, therefore, the school shuts down and everyone's loan was canceled so they did not have to pay it back. However, John Doe missed the opportunity of not having to pay it back because he had just paid his loan off.

Example Two: Jayne Doe starts a new job with several people simultaneously. Everyone is treated kindly and with respect by the trainer. However, Jayne Doe is feeling confused and wondering why she is treated differently like an outcast. She checks herself to see if she is speaking in the proper manner and professionally. She recognizes that she is still experiencing rejection from the trainer. After a while, she continuously has these setbacks and unfair treatment; she becomes confused because she knows she is living a righteous life, believes in Yah, and is filled with the set-apart spirit. However, she keeps running into the same issues. Every time an opportunity for advancement comes, immediately the spirit of rejection shuts it down. Because these evil spirits want her to grow, weary and lose all faith in herself, her dreams, and ultimately her trust in Yah, which is her protection.

Some might ask, **"Can demons take the life of someone prematurely before their time when Yah has the last say so in all things?"** "Yes, they can," I agree that Yah does have the final say in everything; however, Yah will allow **DEATH** to happen to people prematurely because they are sinning against His laws and live very wicked lives, especially when they have been warned and continue willful sin. Yah will also have mercy and compassion on whomever he wants to (**Romans 9:15**). Although it is not within our own efforts, it is Yah's grace and mercy when He blesses us. I would rather not take a chance on not following His laws, and would rather be obedient.

Romans 9:15
"I WILL HAVE MERCY ON WHOMEVER I HAVE MERCY, AND I WILL HAVE COMPASSION ON WHOMEVER I HAVE COMPASSION." [16] So then Yah's choice is not dependent on human will, nor on human effort [**the totality of human striving**], but on Yah who shows mercy [**to whomever He chooses—it is His sovereign gift**]
Sometimes Yah keeps a person and sets them apart to be used for His glory. Therefore, He opens their eyes regarding that evil covenant made with demons so that they can turn and repent from it and break generational curses. People that are handpicked by Yah will generally be used by Yah to learn how to break the curses in their lives and the lives of their families after going through so much hardship and trauma.

The following scripture backs up premature death
Ecclesiastes 7:17. Do not be accessively or willfully wicked and do not be a fool, why should you die before your time?

The names of the following demons are just a fraction of the multitude that roams the earth. Solomon asked the demons their names, and what evil they are responsible for.
33 ELEMENTS OF COSMIC RULER OF DARKNESS: *seven spirits females bound and woven together in one,* fair in appearance and comely; which are the spirits of **deception** (*she deceives and weaves snares here and there*)
http://esotericarchives.com/solomon/testamen.htm

DEMON OF STRIFE: an act of contention: **fight**, **struggle**
DEMON OF ERROR: Causes people to err (*meaning stray; to make a mistake*), causes one to slay their brother. She will lead people into graves and teach them to dig, and she lead errant souls (*errant meaning straying outside the proper path or bounds; moving about aimlessly*) away from all piety (*piety meaning fidelity to natural obligations*), as to parents, and many other evil traits are hers.
DEMON OF BATTLE: Causes the well-behaved individual to scatter and fall foul, causes men to forget their sobriety (**sound mind and calmness**) and moderation (**to become more violent, severe, or intense**). She parts and splits men into parts because strife follows her hand & hand. The meaning of strife is bitter, sometimes violent conflicts. She rends the husband from the sharer of his bed and children from parents and brothers from sisters. The term rend means "to remove from a place by violence:" **WREST,** to split or tear apart or in pieces by force, so, in other words, this spirit comes to destroy all family settings and causes fights and violence in the family.
SPIRIT of **JEALOUSY,** she raises tyrants and tears down kings, and to all rebels, she furnishes power.
DEMON OF WORST: changes their place altogether (*interchange or activate in someone all at once*) but together they live and are woven together. They are known in the world for the term goddesses; this demon says that she is the worst, and she makes a person worse off than they were before because she will impose the bonds of Artemis (*meaning a Greek moon goddess often portrayed as a virgin huntress*).

A Diva Goddess is a Female Demon. Ladies, please stop calling yourselves, and other women Divas. The reference is found in the link below the paragraph regarding the origin of the name and what it symbolizes. Pay attention to the words I typed in bold black. When you are calling each other Divas like it is an honorable word. You are calling each other female demons, and it is not a **DAMN!** Thing honorable about that. Satan always makes things look innocent, **and/or** uses something to make you feel important with a lace of poison behind it. The word **"diva"** became popular in America in the early to mid-nineties. It only takes one person to start something and it catches on. We need to start researching all catchy phrases, fads, and anything that is formed outside of the word of Yah.

The word **"Diva"** came from Italian, which means **"Deity"** (**specifically a female deity: the divine feminine**). Before that, it was the Latin word **"Divus"** (again the divine, **the goddess, the being beyond death**). **"Diva"** hopped over into English usage in the late 1800s.
https://blog.stageagent.com/divas-an-etymology/

Definition of Deity: Supernatural entity beyond the natural being of a human.

If you have accepted and called yourself and other women "Divas." You need to stop and say the following prayer immediately.
Father Yah, I come to you right now in the name of Yahshua with a repenting heart. I am asking for your forgiveness, grace, and mercy for identifying myself with the demon goddess called Diva. I also ask that you forgive me for cursing other sisters by calling them Divas. I renounce, denounce, and reject all that is associated with it in the supernatural and invisible realm. I sever all soul ties and all things internalized in the spiritual realm that I could not see in the physical. I ask that you remove the scales and blinders from my eyes that caused me to be passive about things that I could not see due to the blinders that were placed on my eyes when I made a covenant agreement with that demon.

Now that I have renounced this demon and detached myself from it. Yah I ask that you open the doors that were blocked, and hold up the plans you ordained for my life because I made a covenant agreement with that Diva demon. I declare that this goddess demon called "Diva," no longer has power over my life because I have denounced, renounced, and reject all association with myself and it. In Yahshua's name. Someone called me a goddess and I had to calm myself down and rebuked that statement under my breath. The woman that said it meant no harm because to her it was a compliment of admiration. However, I know the wickedness connected to it the supernatural. Although I know, she did not know any better my skin crawled to call me a goddess. For people that do not know anything about the spirits of darkness in this world, **"goddess"** is looked at, as a **"grand thing."**

DEMON OF BEELZEBUB: Chief demon destroys kings and unites himself with foreign tyrants (*rulers of evil power*). He sends demons that rule over men to influence and eventually believe that they will be lost in the latter end; and the chosen servants of Yah, priests and faithful men. He controls and oppresses them to desire wicked sins, evil heresies (*deny the truth of the scriptures*), and lawless deeds and they obey him instead of the word of Yah. Then he leads them to destruction; inspires men with envy, and desire to murder; influences men to cause wars and engage in sodomy (**to have *oral sex and anal sex with it or the opposite sex***) this spirit likes to be worshipped, brings jealousy and killings in a country, and instigate wars and other evil things, and he proclaims to destroy the world.

DEMON OF ONOSKELIS: "She who has ass's legs (**her legs are shaped like a mule**). This kind of evil spirit is wrought (**to work miracles; bring to the past**). She also strangles men with a noose, she creeps up from nature to the arms, she comes to men in the appearance (**outward and often specious appearance or show**) of a woman, the demon has many characters, **she perverts humans from their true nature (comes upon men and women to make them homosexuals).**

If this kind of demon takes over a person, most likely they were molested or raped by the same sex or opened themselves up to it. However, if the individual was innocent as a child and a victim of molestation or rap for choosing this lifestyle. There is still hope if they renounce this spirit by fasting and praying to be delivered from it. One will have to fast and pray because it is a stronghold. This is one of those demons that does not leave but by fasting and praying. Yah is still a healer and deliverer through Yahshua. Supposed individuals open themselves up to this kind of behavior, by entertaining the thought, and never rebuking it, and decide to go forth with it. In this case, that spirit enters and takes over. This has nothing to do with a gay phobia or hating homosexuals. **DEMONS ARE REAL!** There are scriptures below that back up this paragraph. Its functions are very unnatural, and once this demon enters an individual, they open up the doors for this spirit of same-sex attraction to take over. According to the scripture below, this is wrong and not natural.

Yah gave them over to ***those spirits*** since they did not want to heed his laws or word (**Romans 1:21-32**).[21] [f]or even though [d]they knew Yah [**as the Creator**], they did not [e]honor Him as Yah or give thanks [**for His fantastic creation**]. On the contrary, they became worthless in their thinking [**Yahless, with pointless reasonings, and silly speculations**], and their foolish heart was darkened. [22] Claiming to be wise, they became fools, [23] and exchanged the immortal of Yah's glory, majesty, and excellence. For [f]an image [**worthless idols**] in the shape of mortal man and birds and four-footed animals and reptiles.

[24] *Therefore **Yah gave them over in the lusts of their hearts to [sexual] impurity so that their bodies would be dishonored among them [abandoning them to the degrading power of sin],** [25] because [by choice] they exchanged the truth of Yah for a lie, and worshiped and served the creature rather than the Creator, who is blessed forever! Amein.*

For this reason, **Yah gave them over** *to degrading and* **vile passions
(Romans 1:26-31).**
*Their women exchanged the natural function for that which is
unnatural* **[a duty contrary to nature]**, *In the same way, the men
turned away from the physical role of the woman and were
consumed with their desire toward one another.*
*A man with another man, committing shameful acts and in return
receiving in their bodies the inevitable and appropriate penalty for
their wrongdoing.*

*And since they did not see fit to acknowledge Yah or consider Him
worth knowing* **[as their Creator]**, *Yah gave them over to a depraved
mind, to do things which are improper and repulsive, until they were
filled* **(permeated, saturated)** *with every kind of unrighteousness,
wickedness, greed, evil; full of envy, murder, strife, deceit, malic,
and mean-spiritedness. They are gossipers* **[spreading rumors]**,
slanderers, and haters of Yah. Proud, arrogant, boastful, inventors
[of new forms] *of evil, disobedient and disrespectful to
parents,without understanding, untrustworthy, unloving, unmerciful*
[without pity]. *Although they know Yah's righteous decree and
judgment, those who do such things deserve death, yet they not only
do them, but they even* **[enthusiastically]** *approve and tolerate
others who practice them.*

MEANING OF VILE:

meaningful,nasty,unpleasant, harmful, disagreeable, horrid, horrible
dreadful,abominable,atrocious,offensive,obnoxious,odious,unsavory,
repulsive, off-putting, repellent, revolting Repugnant, disgusting,
distasteful,loathsome,hateful,nauseating,sickening;base,low, mean,
wretched, disgraceful, appalling, shocking, ugly,
Vulgar, sorry, shabby, shameful, dishonorable, execrable, heinous,
abhorrent, deplorable, monstrous, wicked, evil, dark, dirty, vicious,
iniquitous,sinful,corrupt,sordid,depraved,perverted,debased,
reprobate,degenerate,debauched,dissolute,contemptible,despicable,
reprehensible, diabolical, diabolic, devilish, fiendish, hellish,
damnable;yucky,sickmaking,gutchurning,icky,gross,yeah,awful,lowd

own,rotten,sick;beastly, lousy, vomitous;
noisome;scurvy,disgustful,loathly; egregious,flagitious;
Definition of PASSION: strong and barely controllable emotion
DEMON OF ASMODEUS: derived from the Vesta demon, which is a **demon of wrath and arrogance.** Amadeus **plots against the newlywed people** so that they may not know one another (*intimately*).

Turns the spouse against wanting to make love to their husband or wife, to desire to go outside of their marriage to satisfy their sexual needs which causes adultery. This demon causes many calamities, wastes away virgin women's beauty, and arouses (**provokes**), especially mutual enmity or indifference where there had formerly been love, affection, or friendliness in their hearts.

He also transports men into fits of madness and desire (*to be with another woman*) when they have wives of their own so that he leaves them and goes off by night and day to others that belong to other men, with the result that they sin, and fall into murderous deeds (*committed a rash of murders*).

DEMON OF TEPHRAS: the spirit of ashes that is responsible for **bringing darkness on men,** and setting fire to fields; and he brings homesteads (*the home and adjoining land occupied by a family*) to naught (*nothingness*) and the busiest in the summer, but when he gets the opportunity, the demon creeps into corners of the wall, by night and day.
http://esotericarchives.com/solomon/testamen.htm

CHIEF DEMON OF ABADDON-rules over other demons and into speaking spells
DEMON OF ORNIAS: is called "the fierce demon;" likes to consume people's finances and nutrients from the body
DEMON OF OBIZUTH: Demon visits women in childbirth at night, and tries to choke the child; so most likely, this demon causes the umbilical cord to wrap around the baby's neck, as has been reported many times. This demon says if she is unsuccessful, she cannot stop until she is successful; she is a fierce spirit of myriad (**multiple**) names and shapes. She goes here and there, roams to westering parts, and

does her rounds. This demon work is none other than the destruction of children, causes death to their ears (**makes the child die**), and works evil to their eyes (**makes them blind**). She also binds their mouths with a bond and ruins their minds (**making them retarded**), as well as causing pain to their bodies.

DEMON OF WINGED DRAGON: Is a worshiped deity among men, when she chambers (*room; especially: bedroom*), not with many women, but only with a few that are of fair shape (*meaning pleasing to the eye or mind mainly because of fresh, charming, or flawless quality*).

She pairs with them in the disguise of a spirit (*meaning manner, fashion*) winged in form, coitum habens per nates (*Nate meaning buttocks*). Whomever she leaps on that gets pregnant with child, and that which is born of her becomes eros (**eros, meaning to arouse sexual love or desire**) *that particular demon explains why a child I knew of was constantly masturbating since she was six months.*
DEMON OF FIERCE: this spirit is greedy for gold and silver, and hangs over the ocean of water and sea. Then trip up the men who sail thereon, round himself into a wave, and transform himself, then throw himself on ships and land on them. This is his way of getting a hold of money and men; the demon takes the men out of the sea; he does not covet (*desire*) the men's bodies but cast them into the sea. This demon also turns himself into waves and comes up from the sea; this demon sends forth certain nausea (*seasickness*).

DEMON OF LASCIVIOUS: An evil, wicked, lustful spirit; this demon has the form of a man with gleaming eyes and bearing in his hand a blade. This spirit roams in fruitful places, but his daily activity is to seat himself beside the men who pass along among tombs. Untimely in a season, he assumes the form of the dead (*before Yah's time for them to pass away*). If he catches anyone, he destroys him or her with his sword immediately. If he cannot destroy them, he causes them to be possessed by a demon and devour their flesh and hair to fall off their chin.

DEMON OF KLOTHOD: causes battle and makes them well behaved to scatter and fall foul one of the other.

DEMON OF TEPHRAS: Spirit of ashes, brings darkness on men, and set fire to fields; and brings homesteads to naught

DEMON OF BOBÊL (sic): cause nervous illness by my assaults

DEMON OF KUMEATÊL: inflict shivering fits and torpor

DEMON OF ROÊLÊD: causes cold, frost, and pain in the stomach

DEMON OF BULDUMÊCH: separate wife from husband and bring about a grudge between them

DEMON OF NAÔTH: this demon says that he takes his seat on the knees of men **("not sure, what he meant by that, did not go into detail about it, maybe it is arthritis")**

DEMON OF MARDERÔ: send on men with incurable fever

DEMON OF AGCHONIÔN: lie among swaddling clothes and in the precipice

DEMON OF AUTOTHITH: cause grudges and fighting

DEMON OF BIANAKITH: this demon has a grudge against the body, lays waste houses, and causes flesh to decay, and all else, that is similar.

DEMON OF SAPHATHORAÉ: inspire partisanship in men and delight in causing them to stumble

DEMON OF MURMUR/AVENGER SPIRIT: Every time a breakthrough, a blessing, or something significant happens to bless and prosper, the avenger spirit will come and take it. He will rob you of your finances, makes your children go contrary, cause sickness that will bring your peace of mind to chaos, make you feel depressed for no reason, and make it so there will be no one to talk to, will make you feel like nobody cares or wants to be around you **(makes you isolated)**. *Avenger means a person who exacts.*

DEMON OF NECROMANCY: conjuration of familiar spirits of the dead for purposes of magically revealing the future or influencing the course of events.

DEMON OF POVERTY: responsible for keeping someone or families in poverty. *Punishment or inflicting harm in return for an injury or wrong.*

FOX WEDGE DEMON: causes division, the fox represents the demon, and the wedge represents the witch. The wedge fox **(wedge fox imp)** spirit drives a wedge between anything going good.
Kelley, E. Bound to Lose Destined To Win, (2017, pp. 35, 193)

DEMON OF WHIMPEL CLOAK-steals stuff from where you placed it (**works hand & hand with the avenger spirit**).
For example, you lay your keys down and go to another room to get something and return to find the keys gone, the whimpel spirit took it, in hopes that you will say the phrase, "I must be losing my mind," or "I am going crazy;" so that he can start working on taking your mind. Another example is, "say that you put groceries away and you know that you placed a particular thing in the cabinet." However, when you go to the cabinet, it is not there. Therefore, you must command that demon to return your goods.
Kelley, E. Escaping N'Mos Cycle- Volume 1, (2017)

Bible Reference
(Isaiah 3:22) 22 The changeable suits of apparel, and the mantles, and the wimples, and the crisping pins,
DEMON OF N'MOS CYCLE: Takes over and restrains you; a N'mos cycle is an evil spirit that causes a process of repetition for chaos in your life. For example, suppose those in sorcery placed hexes, jinxes, spells, and curses on a person. In that case, they become a jinx to everyone everywhere they go. The cycle never ends. **"Mos" in Latin means "More" (N'Mos Cycle), so there is something that abbreviated a person's life to cause a notorious cycle of more and more chaos to happen over again. "N" stands for** notorious; the meaning of notorious is bad quality or deed, of ill repute, with a bad reputation.

Kelley, E. Escaping N'Mos Cycle- Volume 1, (2017, p.34)
DEMON OF TERRORS BY NIGHT: this spirit keeps people from sleeping at night; influences masturbation and pornography, and causes the demons to infiltrate people
Kelley, E. Terrors By Night (p 9)

(*Psalms 91:5-6 you shalt not be afraid for the terror by night; nor for the arrow that flieth by day;* they rape people in their sleep, they will hold a person down making them feel immobile. Try to pray before you fall asleep; ask Father Yah for sweet sleep. **Proverbs 3:24-25.** When you lie down, you shalt not be afraid: yea, you shalt lie down, and your sleep shall be sweet and not afraid of sudden fear, neither of the desolations of the wicked when it cometh. Also, read the scripture of **Ephesians 6:13-17.** See below the breakdown of this scripture.

*Therefore, put on the complete armor of Yah, so that you will be able to **[successfully]** resist and stand your ground in the evil day **[of danger]**, and having done everything **[that the crisis demands]**, to stand firm **[in your place, fully prepared, immovable, victorious]**.* So stand firm and hold your ground, having [b]tightened the broadband of truth (**personal integrity, moral courage**) around your waist and having put on the breastplate of righteousness **(an upright heart)**, *and having strapped on YOUR FEET THE GOOD NEWS OF PEACE IN PREPARATION **[to face the enemy with firm-footed stability and the readiness produced by the good news]**. Above all, lift the **[protective]** [d]shield of faith with which you can extinguish all the flaming arrows of the evil one and take THE HELMET OF SALVATION, and the sword of the Spirit, which is the Word of Yah.*

DEMON OF F_CK: This is not just a word used for profanity, it is a spirit; each time a person uses this word when swearing, demons are summoned to come to that person. If they have said the "F" word eight times, which is an evil spirit, there will be eight demons in their atmosphere. These demons are angry and want to destroy everything in your life, marriage, finances, and health. Each time a person says, "mother f_ _ _ _ r, they are cursing their mother. When one puts up the middle finger, they are condemning their hand. *Kelley, E. Escaping The N'mos Cycle (2017, p.80-81)*

I got the reference about this particular demon from a man that used to be a wizard/sorcerer (male witch). He gave a remarkable testimony and now is a soldier for almighty Yah after his deliverance. He travels the world, teaching and delivering people from spirits of darkness. He

always talks about how he encountered this spirit called "f_ck" in the worse way. He uses the scripture **Proverbs 5:5** *to describe this evil spirit because he says that each time an individual or group of people say the word f_ _ _.* *This evil spirit called "f"* **comes up the staircase from below the (gates of hell) and will invisibly be in the atmosphere of whoever calls him;** *saying the name f_ _ _ thinking that it is just a word of profanity and not realizing that it is the* **actual name of an evil spirit will destroy your life.** **Proverbs 5:5**: **⁵ Her feet go down to death; her steps take hold on hell.** *Please see the below book I referenced this information.*
Kelley, E. *Escaping The N'mos Cycle (2017, p.80)*

I have learned that this evil spirit brings death to people in many ways, whether by family breakups; killing their morals; dying premature deaths physically; ruining relationships; health failure, finances depleted, and intensifying anger and emotions. Each time this spirit is summoned by someone using the word f_ _ k, it appears and subtracts from that person until the evil spirit eventually kills them, whether physically or spiritually.

Remember that evil spirits come to steal, kill and destroy (John 10:9-10-⁹ I am the door, and anyone who enters through me will be saved [**and will live forever**], and will go in and out [**freely**], and find pasture (**spiritual security**) ¹⁰the thief comes only to steal, kill, and destroy. I came that they may have life and enjoy life more abundantly [**to the fullness until it overflows**].

DEMON OF SH_T: Not just a word used for profanity, but it is also a spirit. **Mr. Kelley** also elaborates on this spirit as well.
DEMON OF BLOCKADE: This spirit blocks you from a prayer life (it has one eye and one arm). He comes to take your mind off prayer and tries to prevent people from getting a breakthrough by throwing all kinds of things in their minds while in prayer.
This spirit will remind you of money you do not have, what is happening against you on the job and who does not like you at work.

Once you get your breakthrough from all the distractions to concentrate and pray, this demon will have people calling you that you have not heard from in a while, something may fall in your house/apartment, and you may start to get sleepy. Someone may start knocking on the door, you may have to go to the bathroom, and the phone continues to ring all of a sudden.

Kelley, E. Bound To Lose Destined To Win (2011, P.191)

If your life identifies with any of the named demons, take it seriously to cast them out of your life. Most likely, you will need to fast and pray for some of them to leave. Some demons are very stubborn, according to *Mathew 9:28-29:*

"Why were we unable to drive it out?" He replied to them, "This kind [of unclean spirit] cannot come out but by fast and prayer [to the Father]. *During that time, the taught ones did not fast, because Yahshua was with them. However, Yahshua did quickly.* The taught ones (**disciples did not start fasting until Yahshua returned to the Father and sent the comforter**).

I highly recommend that you go into prayer and ask Father Yah to lead you into the fast; however, you do not have to wait until you fast to renounce them and cast them out. Do it immediately if you recognize that some of these demons apply to your life. Some of these demons have been in your family for generations. Some refuse to leave unless you fast and pray while breaking the generational curses. I know if you are like me and like to eat; the best fast to start with is with smoothies from 6 am – 6 pm for 3 days or fruit.
The next time, just water unless you are on some kind of medication. However, when you fast, seek Yah's guidance, as long as you are seeking Him in spirit and truth, He will honor whichever fast you choose to start with.

Make sure you have confessed all sins that you can think of.
Forgive people and do not hold grudges, do not hang around people who are not supportive of you, try to mingle with individuals that can pray with you or if going through the same thing, come into agreement and pray for one another or you will be wasting your time.

If you congregate in this way, the process will turn into a team, and the more joined in with a sincere heart in numbers, the quicker the results and less stress on one individual.

The process will be easier because each individual can focus on particular areas and you can all encourage one another. That is why you must be on one occur. Confess all sins and forgive; also repent **(turn from the sin)** with the help of the Almighty. Confess it all to Yah, not holding any grudges, and rebuke all fear and doubt. Also, confess all sins, of ancestors if you know of them. I suggest that you go back as far as seven hundred years. Go to Yah on their behalf and ask for forgiveness of their wicked actions, their sins, rebellion, and iniquities. If you do not know precisely what their sins are, then ask Yah through his Son Yahshua to reveal them to you. Ask family members to tell you some family secrets and things that ancestors or grandparents and parents might have been into, which caused a covenant with those demons to start a bloodline of terror; holding you hostage and holding you back from the blessings of Yah in your life. If you do not find out, you can say the following:

*I renounce, denounce, and reject any blood tie covenants linked to me from evil works and sins caused by my ancestors in the name of Yahshua. (**Specify the name of the demons**), "Now that I know the demon of _______ is causing havoc and curses in my family for generations. You demon of ________I break your powers over my life and my offspring." You also want to command the name of specific demons to leave your territory and bloodline. You should be able to recognize the demons according to their functions and what has happened in your family for generations.*

*I know some of them are hard to pronounce, but do the best that you can, they know whom they are and whom you are talking about, ask the Ruach Ha Quadash (**Holy Spirit**) to be with you and to help you to pronounce it correctly in the spiritual realm on your behalf.*
On the other hand, just say the initial and ask the Ruach Ha Quodesh to speak what the name is for you as you say the initial that causes whatever it is that you need deliverance from. The "F_ck" demon, I would not want to say the word anyway.

The more people in agreement that follow these principles, the more demons will flee and the stronger the deliverance according to the following scriptures:
*One will put one thousand to flight (**meaning the number of demons that will flee**), but two will put ten thousand to flight [**Leviticus 26:8; Deuteronomy 32:30**].* Once you identify the demons that fit the issues in your life and family, if possible, everyone should come together on one occur casting out evil entities from your experiences by renouncing, denouncing, and breaking the curses, covenants, and alters. Then, it will be **MORE POWERFUL!** For example: say it is five of you fasting and praying, touching and agreeing, if two people put ten thousand to flight according to Yah's law, then imagine what five or even three people will do? However, it is crucial not to take this lightly. Everyone must be serious about their deliverance and families, so confessions of their sins to the most high, not carrying grudges and forgiveness must be made, or it is hopeless.

DEMON OF PILLARDOC- This spirit can make people rich by doing crooked and wicked things to get it and can make some people poor. It causes people to become greedy "for the love of money, which the bible refers to it as the root of all evil **(1Timothy 6:10).**
Kelley, E. Bound to Lose Destined to Win (2011, p.143)
DEMON OF BLOCKADE: try to prevent people from praying by sending all kinds of interruptions (*like a phone ring, the baby may wake up and start crying if they were sleeping, a doorbell ring, start getting sleepy, and inappropriate images in mind, making you feel sluggish, or a heaviness comes on you*)
Kelley, E. Bound To Lose Destined To Win (211, p. 191)

DEMON OF BEL: Attaches itself to women; its function is to destroy women. If women experience things like never being able to keep a relationship with the right man, cannot keep a job, teeth seem to fall out for no reason. Always having a hard time, causes pain in the legs, and children are continually growing contrary; feel like a spirit of heaviness on you. It is a "Bel" spirit that has entered your life to cause you to age faster than you should be and makes you lose hair.
Kelley, E. Escaping the N'mos Cycle (2017, p.175)

DEMON OF WASTER/BOOGIE MAN: It keeps people from getting a good night's sleep; it scratches you through the night. People will wake up with bruises, scratches, marks on them, and sometimes bleeding; this spirit will set on your bed **(you can feel your bed go down).** You can feel his presence; it is like the radiation of fear; he will also shake your bed, and they can take on an image of your dead loved one through a psychic or even in the physical. They hate prayer and come into the children's room to haunt them. It causes people to lose money even when Yah answered prayers, **the waster spirit will influence you to do the wrong thing at the right time and vice versa for you to get in trouble;** being out of the timing and perfect will of Yah. The waster spirit will cause you to lose opportunities, privileges, and resources; you may know what to do but cannot seem to get started.

Sometimes you get started but cannot finish, and the waster spirit blocks you from your destiny. Waster makes you look old before your time, breaks down the body, and makes your teeth fall out. My grandmother used to jokingly tell us grandkids that the boogie-man will get us when we do something wrong, not knowing she was summoning this demon to come into our lives to cause harm to us.
DEMON OF BOGEY-Evil spirit that appears at night to scare kids **(which is better known as "boogieman")**
Kelley, E. Terrors by Night (p 10)

DEMON "BIG FACE" –Causes people to join gangs
Kelley. E Bounds to Lose Destined To Win, (2011, pp. 142-143)
RUN AHEAD DEMON- Can dispatch to run ahead of you and cause trouble.
Kelley. E, Bound to Lose Destined to Win (2011, p. 54)

DEMON OF PILLORDAC DEMON-Promises kids fame & power to set them up
Kelley. E Bounds to Lose Destined To Win, (2011, pp. 40,143)

DEMON OF GOMORRA-Makes adults act childish & immature like clowns; also influences people to get plastic surgery; this spirit affects the brain caused by sexual activity outside of marriage. It causes them to forget things they have done moments after they did it **(have nothing to do with Alzheimer's disease or dementia)**. This spirit will make people lose their minds for no medical reason. It also will make them look at themselves as ugly and at the same time, will cause them to become vain and invest in multiple plastic surgeries at any cost. It causes people to become very selfish and promiscuous to feel validated. This spirit affects both males and females negatively. However, it causes the men to get multiple women pregnant to make them feel like they are a man by getting the approval of other men in the neighborhood.
Kelley. E Bounds to Lose Destined to Win, (2011, p.162)

DEMON OF FORNIX-Causes people to become cold-hearted towards others and to murder, whether loved ones or strangers
Kelley. E Bounds to Lose Destined to Win, (2011, p. 163)

DEMON OF PAVOR NOCTURNUS-Kills people in their sleep by choking them to death; this spirit is also responsible for SID **(sudden infant death)**.
Dr. Curtis "Earthquake" Kelley, Escaping the N'MOS Cycle (2017, pp. 199)

DEMON OF WEDGEFOX- Causes division amongst families, friends, spouses, and business partners. It mainly goes after those in authority and where there is trouble brewing. Demons love to shake things up more and tear down the last strain holding them together.
Kelley. E, Bound to Lose Destined to Win (2011, p. 35)

DEMON OF HYDRA HEAD-Very stubborn spirit; described as having the body and tail of a lizard with seven to nine heads. Each one has its personality with its voice. Individuals possessed by this demon are medically diagnosed with schizophrenia and **can never be delivered unless cast out; no medication or psychiatry cures it.**
Kelley, E. Bound to Lose Destined to Win (2017, p.164)

DEMON OF NIKTTIEL-Causes rage, like to intimidate others, and have no self-control
Kelley. E, Bound to Lose Destined to Win (2011, p. 131)
DEMON OF SKYX-Causes Jealousy and Hatred **(this spirit is strong amongst women)**
Kelley, E. Bounds to Lose Destined to Win, (2011, p. 164)

DEMON OF ATARROTH ADDER *("crown of snakes")*-
"This demonic snake wraps itself around a person's head like a crown and slowly squeezes. The spirit squeezes until the person is convinced he can no longer deal with the pressure. Then they kill themselves. The crown of snakes not only attacks homosexuals but also attacks only people engaged in immoral sexual activity. Anybody under so much stress that they feel unable to cope with life is likely dealing with an attack by this demonic spirit. This spirit can also cause migraine headaches."
Kelley, E. Bound to Lose Destined to Win (2011, p. 168**).**

DEMON OF SLOTHFULNESS/PROCRASTINATION: makes you lazy and keep feeling tired and drained; putting off something instead of going forth with it (**to continue to postpone**).
DEMON OF INCANTATION: can either blind you to believing false information about someone or turn you against someone who has done nothing wrong at all, leading you to believe as truth all sorts of lies about him or her.
DEMON OF DISCORD: causes division, bickering, and strife in the family.
DEMON OF SAPHTHOREAL: Causes mental confusion

DEMON OF FAMILIAR: Familiar with you, the spirit that keeps history about you (*Many psychics communicate with this kind of spirit, and that is the reason they can tell you about what is going on in your daily life*), also the monitoring spirit that monitors everything you do.
DEMON OF OPPRESSION: Causes persecution, abuse, and ill-treatment.

DEMON OF HEAVINESS: Causes grief and suicidal thoughts, depression, and never getting over a loved one's death. It comes to the point that the individual does not want to live anymore.
This spirit will whisper in their ear, "you have nothing to live for now," "you might as well just stay in bed and grieve or kill yourself to take away the pain." It causes a person to get depressed for no reason.

DEMON OF DANTOLIEN-Causes people to become bisexual
DEMON OF ALGUL-Vampire demon who lives in cemeteries & enters homes to go after children and kidnap them
DEMON OF ANDRE-Male archdemon who punishes **(torture) people in hell**
DEMON OF ANDREALPHUS-The fallen angel who can transform people into birds, which is witchcraft
DEMON OF ANTAURA-Female demon of Migraine & Serious Headaches
DEMON OF ASELIEL-Male demons who tells demons to appear as beautiful and act loving to deceive you
DEMON OF AMON-Makes people fall in love with the wrong person
DEMON OF ALP-Male demon that causes nightmares and changes into an animal
DEMON OF SAPHTHOREAL-Causes mental confusion
DEMON OF RIX NATHOTO-Causes knee problems (**if there are no medical reasons or physical evidence for being overweight or arthritis, and** doctors cannot find what the problem is, it is this demon), sometimes arthritis is caused by food consumed.
DEMON OF BACUEL-Spirit of pride
DEMON OF BAREGARA-Sits on a rooftop of homes to attack men as they leave
DEMON OF PHARMAKEIA-Demon that causes people to use and abuse drugs and to become addicted to nicotine.

DEMON OF PHANTOM PAIN- Causes a person to feel like something is piercing or stabbing them, and doctors cannot find the problem. **Witches also use this spirit** when they make voodoo dolls in the image of someone and attack them by sticking the doll with pins. This Demon also strikes people to cause them to want to take drugs from the street and constantly depend on prescription drugs. *"Again, I am no doctor, but regarding prescription drugs. I am talking about people wanting to get high on any type of drug, whether through the street or prescriptions."*

"Mr. Kelley stated that he believes the thoughts of homosexuality begin with demonic spirits that attack someone's mind after sexual molestation or experimentation. The enemy will lie to someone and cause that person to have an overwhelming thought that he is homosexual. Demonic spirits will say, "You were born that way." "There is nothing you can do about it, so accept it, and ignore those who tell you that homosexuality is wrong." An overwhelming thought that one is homosexual could come from something as simple as a father mocking his son and calling him a derogatory term that homosexuals use, simply because the son prefers playing the piano over overhunting.

"Demons are listening, and once the seed is planted, the enemy delights in tormenting the son and planning thoughts in his mind that he must be homosexual." Once an individual has been molested, experimented with homosexuality." Even entertained by the thought that they are homosexual, some spirits will gladly attempt to engage the person in that lifestyle.

Kelley, E. Bound to Lose Destined to Win (2011, p. 168).

I also know someone personally that is a homosexual, and he wants deliverance. He loves Yah and stated that he knows what he is doing is wrong but does not know how to be free because it is a stronghold. In addition, a close relative molested him, and his father called him the derogatory name as a child that homosexuals acknowledge. Demons love to get children at a very young age, therefore mothers pray over your baby while in the womb, and once you give birth, continue from there. As parents, we must speak life over our children, not death. There is death and life in the power of the tongue **(Proverbs 18:21).**

DEMON OF REJECTION-Causes people to reject you, whether family members, co-workers, or those in authority over you. You can do something as simple as applying for a particular thing and you are eligible for but because of this spirit of rejection, influencing everyone and everything you encounter, you will be rejected. However, you could be qualified for it. The spirit of rejection will influence the person in authority to disapprove. The one that is not eligible will be approved. No matter how much good you do to others and for others, the opposite happens to you. So it is not always true as many say, those evil things happen to you because of what you did to someone else or you draw certain things to you because that is the way you are is not always the case. One can be good to others and have kindness about them with a loving spirit but the worse always seem to find them and evil people are drawn to them.

Many times, it has to do with a demon that has a right to cause these things because of some covenant made, by either the individual or an ancestor. This spirit wants you to give up hope and develop hate, bitterness, and coldness in your heart over a long period of your life experiencing this. This spirit will make you think of suicide in hopes that you will take your life. Ask me how I know about this so strongly because this spirit of rejection has been haunting me for years. I go into more detail in my book **"<u>Chosen to Break Generational Curses."</u>** This evil demon cause people to be fired from every job for no reason, causes them to do wild things, or they do not have to do anything wrong. The individual can be a hard worker and get along with everyone. Always prompt for work, and never really calls out. However, this demon will give co-workers or supervisors/managers a false perception of the individual causing them to no longer see themselves as good workers. If they are a good worker, the spirit of rejection causes people not to like them for no reason.

Moreover, the supervisors or managers will find a reason to get rid of them or harass them to the point where they will want to quit **(resign)** to save themselves from having a stroke or a heart attack from the stress. This demon hopes that the person they are torturing gets fed up resulting in violence, and rage or they lose their mind for not figuring out why they cannot keep a job when they are doing everything they are supposed to do and volunteered to do more. The spirit of **REJECTION** generally takes over a child's life when they were given up for foster-care, or adoption, or when one or both parents did not want them (**unplanned pregnancies**), and leave them to anybody where they become abused and misused.

For example, the spirit of rejection enters a child when the parent wanted to have an abortion, and although they did not go through with the abortion. The spirit of rejection often enters a child and hijacks the destiny of Yah's plans for their life.

These are examples of how the spirit of "<u>**REJECTION**</u>" operates: When a teacher rejects someone because he/she does not learn as fast as other students do. That individual mind becomes blocked with instability because they cannot concentrate on school due to their basic living environment not being met and the negative experience with the teachers. Most likely they will join gangs and sell drugs with the mentality that they finally are accepted and do not care if they live or die. Unfortunately, this is precisely what the demon of rejection goal is. The spirit of rejection can cause failures in everything, no matter how hard one tries. When people get to that point demons torture them with all kinds of negative thoughts hoping that they will want to end their life; demons come to kill, steal, and destroy **(John 10:10).**

Living an overly wicked life will cause a person's life to end before their time **(Ecclesiastes 7:17). The spirit of rejection can also cause a person's life to end before their time.** By causing heart attacks/strokes, causing bitterness, resentment, rage, and hate to become violent, kill themselves, and kill or be killed.

Marine Demon: lives in the sea, causes ships and boats to capsize, causing big tide waves to overtake and wipe out large grounds of territory and destroy (**as in a tsunami**). It comes in people's dreams to have sex with them to cause a wicked soul tie, causing a perverted marriage in the spiritual realm. This spirit becomes your spouse in the spirit. This spirit can cause the opposite sex to hate you (**causing you never to date**) and claims you as it's own that you belong to him/her like a marriage between to human beings.

For example, suppose you date and both of you like each other. In that case, this spirit will cause your date to have a sudden uneasiness about you, and they will stop calling you, no longer wanting to date you for no reason at all. This spirit can even cause the person you are dating to die physically because it is a jealous demon and resents the strong feelings and attention that you give to that individual. **YES!** This spirit can and has done that, according to former witches that have spoken on this. This spirit also causes people never to get married, or if they do marry it was not the husband or wife that Yah set aside for that person, and they will end in divorce. **Spirit Spouse (is a marine demon):** This demon is very stubborn and aggressive and becomes joined to you through dreams of having sex. Whether it be a form of your own spouse, another person that you know or a stranger. This spirit is joined to you through a forged covenant dream of a sexual encounter. Spiritual Spouses make you feel sexually aroused at any given time, even if no one is tempting you for sex, nor is there anything you are viewing to get you in the mood. You will submit to the intense feeling and masturbate. The spirit spouse does this to keep you from the promises of Yah that He planned for your life. This is also how the spiritual spouse gets sexual gratification through a human willing to submit to masturbation.

A spiritual spouse can keep you from marrying the individual that you are suppose to marry by never meeting him/her or causing intensity between the both of you to not like each other. Suppose everything is great, the both of you click and something deep down inside lets you all know that they are your soul mate. Nevertheless, he/she will just stop seeing you for no reason and it is because of the spiritual spouse that caused it. The spiritual spouse considers you as their own and will cause no one else to have you. They are jealous and feel they have a right to your affection and body only. Therefore, feeling. The spiritual spouse is causing you feel that way because it is ready to have sex with what he/she considers their spouse through masterbation to make love (**to the demon**).

Sex is a pleasurable feeling that was meant for couples that are married as in a woman and man (**huMan**) joined together, not a human and a demon. This spiritual spouse will cause you to have a bad day making you want to do something to make you want to feel good. Whether by drinking alcohol, over eating, using drugs. However, the spiritual spouse will arouse you intensly to want to masterbate. A word called Dopamine is what activates when people have sex bringing on the arousel and orgasms. This spiritual spouse is having sex with you several times a day. Dopamine is the good feeling you get when you have an orgasm and demons know this. When individuals are suffering from some kind of pain or trauma that was never resolved in their life. Masterbation is like a self-medication releasing the Dopamine in the brain to give an individual that temporary satisfaction. Invididuals that are overally sexual driven by a harlot demon having multiple sexual partners are affected in the same way.

The more you engate in it the harder it is to break away from it. Unless you find out how to be delivered from a spiritual spouse. If you have had a spiritual spouse in your life for a long period, and you have just found out how spiritual spouses are joined to you. When you start to work on your deliverance, physical injuries sometimes appear on/and in your body, such as scratches, bites, and symptoms of illness with no medical confirmation. They work hard not to upset Satan; therefore, they prey on your weaknesses and use them against you. They make apparent patterns to attack you consistently on specific dates (**meaning the same things happens every year within the same seasons around the same months**).

How to Get Rid of a Spiritual Spouse:
It is imperative that you break that forged covenant by saying the following. "I renounce, denounce and reject you from being your spiritual spouse that joined with me fraudulently in my dream." "I detach myself from you. "I divorce you and tear up the contract of the marriage certificate in the spiritual realm." "I abort the pregnancy of babies with you." "I kill the children we made in the spiritual realm." "I break every covenant vow made with you in the name of

Yahshua." "I break all powers of incantations, spells, curses, crystal ball use, hex, jinx, voodoo, black majic, marine spirits and hidden things barried with my picture and personal DNA, as in my hair to be up rooted and covered with the blood of Yahshua."

Therefore, you can no longer stand in the way of Yah joining me to be with my earthly spouse set aside for me and our purpose on this earth for Yah's Kingdom. I proclaim this day forward that you no longer have powers to interfere in my life because I have broken that covenant and I am divorced from you indefinantely.
Grant, Z. Be Free From Spirit Spouse (**2017, pp. 12, 13**)
WEATHER DEMONS BY NAME
CHANGO - (prince) controls thunder, lightning, fire

OXUN - god of thunder and lightning.
EUROCLYDON -east wind (**Acts 27:14**) Levant - a surge of the sea, raging, wave
BAAL - god of thunder
SEIR - prince
LEVIATHAN - Job 41:1; Psalm 74:14; Psalm 104:26; Isaiah 27:1
HADADRIMMON - west Semitic storm-god, thunder
URR - Amorite storm god (**Acts 27:14** typhoon wind that came upon Paul at sea).
HURRICANE - means god of evil (**Job 1:19, the whirlwind from the desert that killed Job's children**).

Should we trust using the word "Good Luck?"
"Good Luck" – The words "**good luck**" I believe was created by the dark world of demons, birthed from the ouji board game that was created and made in the state of "**Maryland**" (**Chestertown County**) became a popular game in 1890. On April 25, 1890. An individual called "**strong medium**" that was visited by the creator of the game to do a seance when the game was made but was not sure what to call it. They asked the "**strong medium.**" The medium turned to the board and asked what it wants to be called and it spelled out "**O-U-I-J-A**" and when they asked what that means, the board spelled out "**G-O-O-D- L-U-C-K.**" Therefore, it is not good to say to someone "**good luck.**" You might cursong them in some way. As far as we know the word "**luck**" could mean curse. Satan always have a lie mixed with truth. The word good seems innocent and "**good**" right? However, it is no telling what the word "**luck**" means.

Because spirits of darkness revealed that is what the name of its board game means. **I DO NOT TRUST IT!!** Satan and spirits of darkness can give people ideas and words to implement. Therefore the individual that was lead to start putting those words together could have been used by Satan to introduce "good luck."

The building where the séance happened is still there, 529 N. Charles Street. It is a 7-Eleven.
https://time.com/4529861/ouija-board-history-origin-of-evil/

EXAMPLE PRAYERS FOR FREEDOM

NOTE: Before you do this, put on some praise and worship music and lift your hands to give Yah sacrifice praises whether you feel like it or not. Scripture says that praise confuses the devil, and Yah inhabits the praises of his people (**Psalms 22:3**).
DO NOT LET HOW YOU FEEL STOP IT! Do it anyway, even if the flesh does not want you to.

Father Yah, I come to you through the name of your Son Yahshua with repentance and asking for forgiveness, mercy, and grace. Now that I know the truth, I want to be free, please forgive me for being a part of demonic activity in ignorance. Now that I have the knowledge and understanding of these practices, I repent of them. Thank you for not allowing evil spirits of darkness to take my life before my time and die in my sins to face hell for eternity. I ask that you deliver me from all curses, spells, and evil altars set up for my destruction. Please forgive me for believing and practicing that hidden wickedness and breaking all curses in my life associated with it. I ask that the Holy Spirit will guide me into all truth from now on as I read your laws on how I am supposed to live.

Suppose you are not ignorant of these practices but engaged in wicked activities because you enjoyed it, and no longer want to because you have learned the truth. You need to repent of it before Yah **IMMEDIATELY!** Say to Yah that you repent and no longer want to be a part of Satan's kingdom because it will lead you to the **"LAKE OF FIRE,"** and you do not want to be in an eternity of damnation.

SPEAK THIS OUT ALOUD TO THOSE DEMONS YOU HAVE IDENTIFIED WITH THAT AFFECTED YOUR LIFE:

Now that I know who you are (**name the specific demon**), I renounce, denounce, and reject you. I cancel every covenant made with you that opened a doorway for you to come into my life and dictate my destiny.

I command that the altar made to perform witchcraft against me crumble and be destroyed. Every evil word spoken against me to cause jinx, hex, incantations, and curses in my life, which I cast to the ground. All evil alters made to perform, blood sacrifices, voodoo, black magic, enchantments, incantations, and harm against me. I destroy it calling down the invisible fire from the third heaven. In Yahshua's name, I declare that all is destroyed first in the spiritual realm and no longer be active in the physical realm. Father Yah, I ask that you eradicate all curses, spells, and evil alters that have been canceled and destroyed that I have spoken.

Everything that has me tied down spiritually I break the covenants, invisible ropes, and strings that have me bound and hogtied, whether I did it on my own or they were caused by witchcraft, voodoo, or curses through my bloodline ancestors. I am asking that Yahshua, Yah's son, who became a curse for me when he was hung at the stake, intervene in my life and break the penalty of the curses and the consequences.

I break all powers and destroy all covenants made against me. I cancel every covenant and contract made out of ignorance and I declare that these evil forces no longer afflict me, no longer have a right to exercise power to destroy my pathway for the purpose that I was born to do, and make a difference in the Kindom of Yah for His Glory. Yah, your law declares in **Proverbs 22,** that the curse can only come if there is a cause. I am asking that the fire of the **Ruach Ha Quadash (Holy Spirit)** uproot and dig up all roots of evil working against my family and me. Father Yah, I now transfer those curses placed upon my family and me to your son Yahshua, who has become a curse for me on the stake to proclaim the deliverance he shed His blood for your chosen people.

Father Yah, send your healing power through your son Yahshua. Father Yah. If you need to lead me to a fast that will give me healing power for this kind of breakthrough from dark forces lead me, or send someone in my life that is filled with the truth of your laws that have a personal relationship with you, and knows-how to fight spiritual warfare to assist me. **Father Yah, no longer will I sit back and accept all that is wrong in my life for the rest of my life**. Your law states that your thoughts of me are good and not of evil and to have peace and an expected end **(Jeremiah 29:11)**.

Your law says that you wish that I prosper in every area of my life. Therefore, Father Yah with the authority you have given me according to **Luke 10:19**, I break the powers of every invisible rope and chains that have tied me down spiritually, everything that is fighting against me in the spiritual realm that has caused me not to walk in the things of the spirit and think properly. Everything that is speaking against my destiny I command that you shut your mouth in Yahshua's name. Yah I ask that you seal this denouncement by eradicating everything I have just spoken, including all forged covenants in my life, in Yahshua's name.

Definition of Eradicate- putting an end to something

Spirit of Fear, I renounce, denounce, and I harshly reject your presence and command that you leave my dwelling space. I disassociate myself from you, and I divorce you from my life. I refuse to be a co-conspirator to myself and every covenant made in error for lack of knowledge and verbal participation. I reject, denounce, and renounce all association with it. Either by dreams from the spiritual realm or the physical realm. I break the chains of all shackles to release me from all bondage in the name of YAHSHUA. Father Yah, whatever I have done to endorse this, I divorce that spirit, I separate my soul from the curses and sever the cords in the spiritual realm to be free in the physical realm.

I cancel every curse and I break the power of the gate altar made to tie me to invisible cords, discord, and restrictions. I command silence to every voice speaking against my family and me; I break every curse and sorcery against me. I tear down every tower made and built over the years by adding more curses to destroy my destiny and life. **Father Yah, I believe that you are in agreement with me when I command that whatever Satan's agents planted to attach itself to me**, I send it back, in the name of Yahshua. I command confusion in their camp; I command that every demon return to their dwelling from hell and turn against each other. I declare that their altars fail, brought to disgrace and open shame so that Yah's people see that there is no power higher than the power of Yah.

Hebrews 13:15-16 (Sacrifice of Praise to Yah)
Through Him, therefore, let us at all times offer up to Yah a sacrifice of praise, which is the fruit of lips that thankfully
acknowledge and confess and glorify His name. [16] *Do not neglect to do well, to contribute [**to the needy of the assembly as an expression of fellowship**], for such sacrifices are always pleasing to Yah.*
MEANING OF INHABIT: 1: to occupy as a place of settled residence or habitat; to be present in or occupy in any manner or form

BACK TO EXAMPLES OF PRAYERS
I cancel and break every evil covenant and spell against me by using personal items of mine, such as pieces of clothing and pictures that have disappeared, hair, and fingernails that were stolen that hold my DNA to lay on evil altars. Just like Elisha called down fire from the third heavens. I call down the invisible fire from the third heavens to destroy the gate altar in the invisible realm that was made to speak to my demise.

I break the same patterns that occur every year because of the designated timeframes of a cycle to keep me delayed and going forward like a repeated circle. I break and dismantle that pattern that occurs every year at the same time to make trouble on my job. I cancel every attack and break the powers of evil off my finances and all evil attacks that cause family members to come against me. All is working out for my good to give Yah the glory. I break and cancel every curse

at that evil gate altar. I send the invisible fire in the spiritual realm
from the third heavens down on the gate altar to consume it, destroy
it, and turn it to ashes. I seal with the blood of Yahshua.

PLEASE NOTE: Some family members and people you have
known for years, and old friends are meant to be absent in your life
because of your call; otherwise they can be a hindrance. Therefore,
ask Yah to show you and confirm why he wants certain family
members and friends to be distant from you. **For example,** it could
be that they do not respect or accept your call, refuse to support you,
and will hate seeing you blessed. Yah know they will be a weight or
setback in your life.

Father Yah, based on all the knowledge I have received, I
internalize it into my spirit, invigorate my soul, give me the power to
spring forth, and begin to put your laws in my heart to bend to your
will. Put your principles, precepts, commandments, and protocols
into action to receive the promises that you have made for me before
the foundations of the world. I now speak against every evil altar,
satanic sacrifice, and covenant that my ancestors have made from
lack of knowledge. I break, dismantle, and destroy it with the
invisible fire that I call down from the third heavens. I command that
it all be consumed through the Holy Spirit fire, every decree written
by my ancestors, every law, every rule, and every injunction made
covertly in my life through the commitments, allegiance, covenants,
and agreements made by my ancestors. Whether by **Freemasonry,
Secret Societies, voodoo, witchcraft, sorcery, Fraternities,
Sororities, Yoga meditation, sage smoke, and prayers.** Whatever
they did, father Yah, that forged covenants with demons and oaths
that were made with demon entities to come into binding agreements,
and contracts that put my life in a bind, and the offspring of my
bloodline. I cancel, break and destroy it in the name of Yahshua.

**Father Yah, just like Elijah called down the fire from the third
heavens. I call your invisible fire down from the third heavens to
destroy all evil altars set up to speak curses against me.** In faith, I
call down the invisible fire from the third heavens to destroy every

spiritual and physical altar that has delayed me to meet and marry the spouse that you have anointed for me to go forth in marriage. I divorce all spiritual spouses that were joined by covenant dreams. I murder renounce, reject and denounce all spiritual children conceived from the spiritual spouse. I disconnect myself from them and sever every soul tie made in the spiritual realm that activated in the physical realm.

I renounce and reject what was internalized to form soul ties. Now that I am divorced and disconnected in the spiritual let it manifest my freedom in the physical. I call the invisible fire from the third heavens down on that evil gate altar that caused a lack of finances and setbacks. I command that the invisible fire from heaven destroy every demonic area of my life that hinders me from my blessings.

I command that every witch be silenced and Satan's agents are stopped immediately in the name of Yahshua.

Every evil altar speaking against my bloodline, from both sides of my mother and father's side as far back ten centuries of generations, to the current. In the invisible realm, I tear up every contract and license that gave them authority to torture, curse, and cause destruction in my life. In the name of Yahshua, I command destruction by the fire of the Holy Spirit. I send the angelic host of Father Yah to destroy every altar. My child, grandchildren, and generations forward will not suffer as I did from unknown curses and spells because of associated demons. I declare that my bloodline shall no longer be affected by any evil altars again nor those that try to come against any of my descendants in the future. I command that the agents sending reinforced curses and spells, backfire and become consumed by their own evil they are projecting at my descendants, let the law of scripture be their portion that says, "those that curse me, Yah will curse those that curse me" (**Genesis 12:3**).

Father Yah, I pray that every soul tie of setback, waster spirit, blocking spirit, spirit of rejection, and poverty is a day of deliverance today. Let this be the day of restoration from years of what the locust, cankerworms, and palmer worms have eaten in my life through sorcery; let it come to an end in Yahshua's name. I thank you Father Yah for giving me the spirit of knowledge, and wisdom and for revealing revelations to me.

BELOW I WANT YOU TO ENTER WHATEVER DEMON FITS YOUR SITUATION IN THE SPACE OF THE PRAYER TEMPLATE

I renounce, denounce, and cast out the root and Chief demon of
_____________, _____________, _____________, _______________ and all
sub-demons. I bring you into captivity and submission to the laws of Yah with the power that Yah has given me, to trample over scorpions and serpents. I paralyze you in the spirit from interfering in my life. I speak against every hex, witchcraft, jinx, black magic, incantation spirit, and pledge made. I come against voodoo acts, and yokes placed upon my family and me, and for bondages to be broken, in the name of Yahshua. Father Yah, now that I have cast out those spirits. I ask that you give me the spiritual eyes to see beyond smiles and sweet talk in the physical realm and amplify my gift of discernment to detect these things. I ask that you eradicate every spell, curse, and evil altar that was broken by the command of my lips.

Now I ask that the angelic host of Yah be assigned to me to go forth and perform the laws of Yah according to **Psalm 91:11-12.** According to the law written in **Isaiah 54:7,** I say, no weapon formed against me shall prosper, and every evil tongue that rises against me to hold me back from my blessings, I condemn it in the name of Yahshua with his laws.

Now that I have gone forth, I proclaim that this day my blessings will embrace me, and Yah will point me in the direction where I am supposed to be at this time in my life. I now declare that there will be no more delays. There will be no more setbacks; from the chief spirit "procrastination," it shall not prosper.

The spirit of defeat and the spirit of incompetence are bound. I bind all powers, and I release the spirit of advancement.
Father Yah, slingshot me to where you ordained me to be at this time in my life. In the mighty name of **Yahshua,** I bind and paralyze

demonic spirits that dwell on the earth assigned to hinder my family members and me in Yahshua's name. Furthermore, I use the name and blood of Yahshua to destroy and nullify demonic and satanic agreements between rulers of darkness in high places and occultism or demonic forces of the earth fashioned against my family members and me in Yahshua's name.

In the name of Yahshua, I declare this power of promises according to the laws of Yah to activate. I command all my blessings and potentials buried by wicked and household enemies to be exhumed. I declare that no blessing that Yah has attributed to me this year will pass me by. Father Yah, just as Abraham received favor in your eyes, I ask that you grant me the same.

My blessings will not be transferred to my neighbors this year because I am delivered from the spirit/spirits of rejection,________,________,________. Father Yah, cast down every demon power that is out to detour your program for my life, in the name of Yahshua.

Every Chief Demon of __________ and sub-demons. I am confronting you from my position of authority, according to **Isaiah 54:17**. I release the invisible consuming fire of Yah, and I call down the fire from the third Heavens just as Elisha did in the physical to destroy every target that has my name on it in your camp. I command that all alters that are set up to destroy me are now destroyed! In the mighty name of Yahshua

Father Yah, I ask that you send Michael, your most powerful warring angel, to attack the spirits of darkness that are on my trail. I send hailstorms upon every head of every demon. I send an invisible earthquake into the enemy's camp to destroy and bring down every satanic altar that has been set up against me, and my family loved ones, my ministry, gifts and the fruits of my spirit, my finances, and all that belong to me. In the name of Yahshua.

I take back everything that was hijacked, my sound mind, my personality, my perfect health with no diseases, my boldness and courage in Yah to stand up for what's right no matter who or what I may lose along the way. Right now, I bind and destroy any demonic powers that are trying to take over my mind, my peace, and my heart. I dismantle it all in the name of Yahshua.

Yah, show me how to be a blessing to your people, as you open my spiritual eyes to the understanding of your Laws, in Yahshua's name. I refuse to accept and operate in fear in my life. I uproot any and everything that is not of the Kingdom of Yah in the name of Yahshua. Yah, through your son Yahshua, please reveal to me everything that is hidden in the spiritual realm. Ruach Ha Quodesh (**Holy Spirit**), help me to discern the things that I do not understand and cannot see in Yahshua's name.

Yah, show me how to be a blessing to your people as you open my spiritual eyes to the understanding of your Laws, in Yahshua's name. I reject every evil report, infirmity, and loss of a job that is trying to bring fear into my life I destroy it in Yahshua's name.

In the name of Yahshua, remove every spiritual distraction and scales from my eyes that have blinded me from seeing in the Spirit. Father Yah, we are in this battle and agreement that your consuming fire will burn down every blockage, bondage, roadblock, and satanic wall that the enemy has built against me, and I command it to be destroyed in the name of Yahshua

SCRIPTURES TO LEARN AND MEDITATE

Leviticus 26:40-42: (40) But if they confess their iniquities and the iniquities of their fathers, with their trespasses, in which they trespassed against Me. Also walked contrary to Me, (41) and that I also have walked contrary to them and have brought them into the land of their enemies. Suppose their uncircumcised heart is humbled, and they accept the punishment of their iniquity, (42). In that case, I shall remember my covenant with Jacob and Isaac. Also, remember My covenant with Abraham, and remember the land, father; you said that
you would give the one that repents mercy, so here I am asking for

your mercy and to be set free from the evils of the alters that have been running their course in my life. Father Yah, you said in your word that those who hide their sins should not prosper, but he who confesses their sins and forsake themselves, mercy shall come. I now believe that I have mercy and prosper because I confessed my sins and repented.

Isaiah 54:7- therefore I say, no weapon formed against me shall prosper and every evil tongue that rises against me, I condemn it in the name of Yahshua

Proverbs 4:7 –The beginning of wisdom is: Get knowledge! Moreover, with all your getting, get understanding.

Ecclesiastes 7:17 [17] Do not be excessively *or* willfully wicked and do not be a fool. Why should you die before your time?

Mathew 10:36 – A man's enemy will be those of his household when one believes, and another does not.

Psalms 8:2; 44:13: Out of the mouths of infants and nursing babes, you have established strength because of your adversaries. That you may silence the enemy *and* make the revengeful cease.

Psalms 44:16: Because of the voice of the taunter and reviler, because of the presence of the enemy and the avenger

Isaiah 54:15-"If anyone fiercely attacks you, it will not be from Me. Whoever attacks you will fall because of you.

Proverbs 24:17

Do not rejoice *and* gloat when your enemy falls,
and do not let your heart be glad [**in self-righteousness**] when he stumbles,

Proverbs 24:33-34

"Yet a little sleep, a little slumber, a little folding of the hands to rest [**and daydream**],"
[34] then your poverty will come as a robber, and your want will be like an armed man.

Exodus 22:18 you shall not allow a woman who practices sorcery to live (**Amplified version**)

Thou shalt not suffer a witch to live (**King James Version**)

Proverbs 26:2 as the bird by wandering, as the swallow by flying, so the curse cause shall not come. (**KJV version**). The sparrow in her

wandering, like the swallow in her flying, so the curse without cause does not come *and* alight [**on the undeserving**] (**Amplified version**)
Psalms 109:1-17 He also loved cursing, and it came [**back**] to him; He did not delight in blessing, so it was far from him.
Psalms 109:1-3
O Yah of my praise! Do not keep silent, ² for the mouth of the wicked and the mouth of the deceitful are opened against me; they have spoken against me with a lying tongue.³ they have also surrounded me with words of hatred. They have fought against me without a cause.
Psalm 144:1 blessed be Father Yah, my Rock, *and* my great strength,

who trains my hands for war and my fingers for battle;
Hebrews 12:29 our Yah is a consuming fire
Numbers 23:19- Yah is not a man that should lie
Romans 8:37 I am more than a conqueror
Deuteronomy 28:13 I am the head and not the tale
Philippians 4:13 I can do anything through Yahshua that strengthens me
Psalms 50:15 call on me in the day of trouble: I will rescue you, and you shall honor and glorify me.
Jeremiah 23:29 is not my word like fire and like a hammer that breaks
Revelations 12:12 Woe to the earth and the sea, because the devil has come down to you in great wrath, **knowing that he has *only* a short time [remaining]!"**
Philippians 2:9 for this reason also [**because He obeyed and so completely humbled Himself**], Yah has highly exalted Him and bestowed on Him the name which is above every name,

2 Corinthians 10:3-5
For though we walk in the flesh [**as mortal men**], we are not carrying on our [**spiritual**] warfare according to the flesh *and* using the weapons of man. ⁴ The weapons of our warfare are not physical [**weapons of flesh and blood**]. Our weapons are divinely powerful for the destruction of fortresses. *We are* destroying sophisticated arguments and every exalted *and* proud thing that sets itself up against the [**true**] knowledge of Yah. W*e are* taking every thought *and* purpose captive to the obedience of Yahshua, being ready to punish every act of disobedience when your obedience [**as a church**] is complete.

SUMMARY

Please be mindful that Satan and demons come to **Still, Kill and Destroy!! (John 10:10)**. We need to seek as much knowledge as we can with the leading of the Ruach (**Holy Spirit**) because He leads us to all truth. I say that because there are so many doctrines out here that have truth mixed with lies which is a trick of Satan that will lead you to strange doctrines down a road of destruction as the bible says **Hebrews 13:9**. You need to be rooted and grounded in the truth (**James 1:6-8**) so that you will not be tossed around like waves in the sea to and fro. When the children of Yah are not aware of how to fight Satan and demons with the two edge sword (**Yah's laws in the bible**) that he/she has access to fight those demons successfully to resolve all problems and issues, and errors of their ways. Nevertheless, they will perish for the lack of knowledge. Yah says in his word that my people perish for the lack of knowledge (**Hosea 4:6**).

Perish does not always mean to die physically. However, one can die within their soul, mind, and spirit. Whatever is draining that individual, they do not know how to resolve it without the knowledge of Yah. Moreover, that will cause their mind to go into desperation mode, irrational thinking, fear, anger, bitterness, and rage. Because they do not have Yah's knowledge from His word embedded in their heart to arrest them and not let them fall into dispair and make harsh decisions.

"My people perish for the lack of knowledge." To perish means all hope is lost, it seems to be no way out, and with all the sickness and stress on their mind, heart, and soul. The body can and will perish too. Meaning heart attack, stroke, high blood pressure, etc. Satan and demons are depending on your lack of knowledge. The more you are not aware of Yah's knowledge, the more your lives are detoured from the plans Yah has set for you according to His purpose for your life. Satan will use the things of this wicked world to usurp the way you think and make decisions if you are not aware of the laws of Yah as to what you are to do in this journey called **"life,"** according to his word. We are always in a spiritual battle and when we are children of Yah, He has given each of us gifts for His kingdom, and we use it to fight Satan and his demons kingdom, which cannot prevail against the weapons of Yah that he gives his children to fight with.

REFERENCES

I encourage you to visit the websites and purchase every book below. In addition to what I have learned through the Holy Spirit about spiritual warfare on my own. The following authors below were also an influence on me. I highly recommend their books.

The Testament of Solomon-Pine.com (n.d).
http://ww.piney.com/ApocTestSolom.html
Merriam-Webster's Online Dictionary
https://www.merriam-webster.com/
Bible Gateway Online
https://www.biblegateway.com/versions/Amplified-Bible-AMP/
(www.pixabay.com)
Licensed Free Graphics for the public to use from the Pixabay website

---

BOOK RECOMMENDATIONS

Earthquake Kelley, "Bound To Lose Destined To Win" (2011)
https://www.alibris.com/Bound-to-Lose-Destined-to-Win-Earthquake-Kelley/book/184...
Kelley, E., Escaping N'Mos Cycle- Volume 1, (2017)

Earthquake Kelley, The Dangers of Profanity "Stop Cussing," (2019)
*Earthquake Kelley (**former sorcerer/warlock**) stated, "The Haitian witch, who taught him voodoo had a better understanding than most Christians of how we are shaped in iniquity. She taught him that low-level demonic spirits dwell in every hospital and wait for children to be born. The spirit grabs the head of the baby, right alongside the person who is delivering the baby. A demonic spirit is assigned to each child, and the job of this spirit is to teach the child to do evil. First and foremost, it teaches the child to lie, then to cheat and steal." Psalm 58:3 says the wicked are estranged from the womb; they go astray as soon as they are born, speaking lies. This demonic spirit even has a classroom, and where do you think it is? Right there in your child's room, especially at night."*

Dr. Olusola Coker, "1000 Prayers against the Activities of Witchcraft" (2018)
https://us.diebuchsuche.com/book-isbn-9781539442998.html

Pastor UzorNdekwu, Overthrowing Evil Altars, (2015)
John Eckhardt, Prayers That Rout Demons
Zita Grant, Be Free From Spirit Spouses (2017)

There are more than sixty-six books of the Bible because many were removed. The edition of *Pseudepigrapha/Book of Solomon (Old Testament)* is one of the so-called lost books I used to reference the listed names of demons and their duties.

Please contact me via email at tearsformysisters3588@gmail.com to tell me how this book helped you and your family.

The following are additional books I have written that can be found on Amazon:
"Tears for My Sisters"; **"Prophetic Poetry" My Gift To You**; **"Sequel of Prophetic Poetry"** and **"Who Are The True Chosen People of Yah"**
There are also several Journals listed as well in Amazon that I designed and made for devotional time.

Please also visit my YouTube Channel: **"Warriors for Yah."** There are several channels with that name. However, my channel is the one with the flower and butterfly. Also, **Pastor Kevin Ewing** has a YouTube channel that teaches about Spiritual Warfare.

Make sure that you drop me an email to let me know how this book enlightened you and how it helped you. Once I receive your email I will have you on my list to let you know when I have released other books. Also, type my name in the search box of Amazon to see all books I have written. You can also type in my name on google search box and some of my books will populate. Also, bookstores to purchase my books if you do not want to use Amazon. I look forward to hearing from you all.

Shalom